– DART –
The Magical River
—KEN DUXBURY—

BEST WISHES

from

Ken Duxbury

BOSSINEY BOOKS

First published in 1987
by Bossiney Books
St Teath, Bodmin, Cornwall
Designed, typeset and printed in Great Britain by
Penwell Ltd, Parkwood, Callington
Cornwall

ISBN 0 948158 31 X

PLATE ACKNOWLEDGEMENTS

Front cover by Ken Duxbury
Page 75 Mark S Wilkins
Pages 94, 98 R E Jones
Pages 90, 93 Britannia Royal Naval College,
Dartmouth
All other photographs, drawings and maps
by the Author.

Front Cover: Ann Lomax at Holne Bridge on
the River Dart.
Back Cover: Dartmouth Castle and St Petrox
Church.

Contents

About the Author and the Book

Ken Duxbury has an unusually rich experience of outdoor adventure, having been introduced to an aquatic life by twelve years service in the Royal Navy. There, as an officer he gained command of one of HM Ships before retiring in 1954 to found a highly successful sailing school on the north coast of Cornwall.

Scorpio is his watery astrological sign, so it is not surprising that his whole life has been involved with rivers and the sea. Author of twelve books, he started writing in 1957 and has been boating columnist for the *Sunday Express* for thirty years.

Sea Stories of Cornwall, his first best-selling book for Bossiney, was published in 1984 followed by an equally successful *Coastline of Cornwall* in 1985. *Dart* forms his 'hat-trick' for this Cornish cottage publisher.

In the book he recaptures—much of it from his kayak canoe—that elusive quality of magic first experienced as a child while exploring another inland river on whose banks he grew up. To quote Ken's own words: 'It was there I gained my deep regard for the beauty and harmony of nature, for that was a truly enchanted world and it left an indelible mark on my soul. Though the Dart is very different from that river of my childhood; far more elemental and aware of its destiny from the start, writing this book has reawakened the thrill of that half-forgotten knowledge. There is adventure ahead!'

Left: What better way to explore a river?
The author in his 15 foot kayak.

The Magical River

I was born and brought up on the leafy banks of a river.

My deep regard for the beauty and harmony of nature springs from many childhood hours spent roaming that river's banks, or peering with bated breath into some tranquil rush-filled pool, hopeful of detecting a dark form or perhaps the finny flick of a tail. My brother and I spent hours, indeed days, floating down with the current on flimsy home-made rafts, half dry and half safe but wholly

Below: Dartmeet: wonderful for the family picnic.

Right: 'I learned the way of the current as it sweeps round a bend.'

Kingswear Castle, now a private residence.

captivated by adventures which befell, until a fallen elm maybe—for England was then a country of elms—barred further voyaging. It was there I awakened to a contained perception of pure magic.

That was a truly enchanted world and it left an indelible mark on my soul. I am grateful to that river. On it I learned the way of a current as it sweeps round a bend, and where to look for a pike, roach, gudgeon or dace, for I found that each fish seeks out a subtly different quality in the water or the river bank. Unwittingly I discovered those qualities; the distinctive look and feel of gravel and stones that the shallows have scoured bright with a quickened flow, or the treachery of smooth rock where the current has grown indolent, allowing growth of a green patina of weed or moss. And the fathomless—ah, how fathomless they seemed!—dark pools under the willows where shafts of a myriad bullrushes plumbed the depths. They whispered secretly in their tops as they quivered at the unknown things which fingered their toes down there where no light penetrated.

So I came very early in life to know a river intimately, and writing this book has re-awakened the thrill of that half-forgotten knowledge. I am obliged to Michael Williams for being the catalyst in that re-awakening.

Dart has been the instrument.

The Dart is a very different river from that one of my childhood: far more elemental, more astringent I think and aware of its destiny from the start. But is this not just part of the magic of rivers? Like we humans no one of them, thank heaven, is the same as any other.

There is adventure ahead.

The weir near Buckfast.

WEST and EAST DART

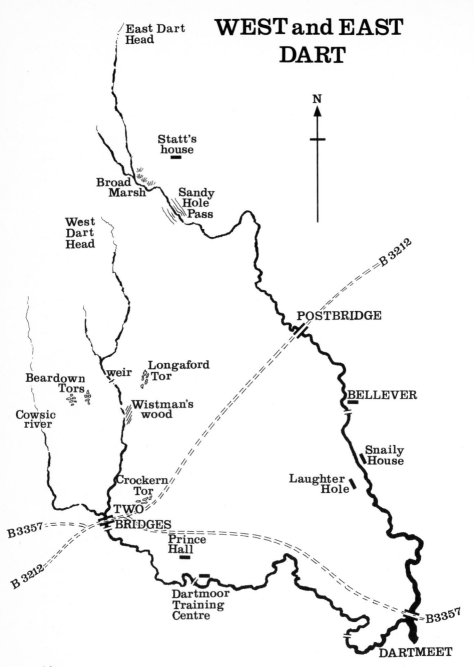

East Dart Head

N

Statt's house

Broad Marsh

Sandy Hole Pass

West Dart Head

B 3212

POSTBRIDGE

weir

Longaford Tor

Beardown Tors

BELLEVER

Wistman's wood

Cowsic river

Snaily House

Crockern Tor

Laughter Hole

TWO BRIDGES

B3357

Prince Hall

B 3212

Dartmoor Training Centre

B3357

DARTMEET

I
West Dart

I cannot tell what ye say, brown streams,
I cannot tell what ye say.

Charles Kingsley

Some of us may think that rivers just 'happen'.

I prefer to think of them as being born—born that is from a union of two elements, rain and the earth. Is it not also true that, as with a human being, the character of a river is indelibly stamped on it by the nature of its birthplace and early life? It seems to me that this unique and distinguishing imprint stays with a river in some magical way throughout the whole journey until it flows as a deep and perhaps navigable torrent back into the ocean.

The countryside through which it passes is modified by, and in turn modifies, a river so that again as with a human being there is a complex inter-relationship at work during the whole lifetime. One final human analogy: sometimes those creative forces which give birth to a river spring a surprise and produce twins!

So it is here in the heart of Dartmoor, for this River Dart starts some 1,800 feet above sea level as two separate southward-running streams: East and West Dart. Though you may search the whole of the British Isles, I think you will not find a place where you will experience a more profound sense of contact and involvement with those raw creative elements of earth and sky. Up here where the twins are born one is likely at any moment to be enveloped in the very clouds which give these two trickles of peaty water their first moist breath, and it would be an insensitive mortal who remains unaware of the awe-inspiring massif of the Moor underfoot, whose name is linked with the river it spawns.

Some 290 million years ago this craggy mound of granite which is now Dartmoor thrust up as molten magma from Earth's heart. Since then glaciers have scoured its surface; wind and rain have eroded its crust and eaten into the rock to form the many shallow upper moorland valleys, shorn of all adornment, that we see today.

This high moor is a watershed. Within a very short distance of the two sources of the Dart the River Tavy starts its slightly more westerly course to join the mighty Tamar at Plymouth, and the rivers Bovey and Teign trickle off in a more easterly direction to Newton Abbot. From the same area the East and West Okement rivers start their career northward to join the Torridge which flows into the Bristol Channel at Bideford. A multitude of other small brooks and tributaries have their origin in this area, each to link with others and finally flow more or less north or south to the sea.

On a geological time scale Man has been on the scene for barely the flicker of an eye. First traces tell us that a mere ten thousand years ago Mesolithic nomads were ranging the Moor, but Man first took up residence on the upper banks of the Dart some 4,000 years back, and the actual name *Derte* appears first to have been written down in 1080 AD, pinned to it by early Saxon settlers. But the river, of course, was old long, long before our consciousness gave it recognition. At the start they are close twins, these two streams, for less than one mile separates the West Dart from her sister which comes into being some two miles farther north. They then diverge a little to retain their separate identities for about ten miles before deciding that union is the better part, and Dartmeet is the well-named point of their fusion.

Both sources lie close under the bare and rounded contours of Cut, Whitehorse and Black Hills which you may easily locate on the excellent Ordnance Survey 'Outdoor Leisure' map number 28 available from any good bookshop. You are ill-advised to roam up here unless you are experienced, carry and know how to use a compass, and have company, for a sudden mist may wipe out every distinguishable feature. Quite apart from the numerous treacherous bog patches, you might then accidentally stray into one of the Military Danger Areas, having missed the warning Range Notice-boards which are dotted around. These alert one to the exercise firing grounds which lie largely to the west and north—a necessary evil, alas, which is likely to remain with us until the babe Homo Sapiens matures from his crèche.

12

The first trees on the higher moor.

Some two and a half miles from its source the West Dart has already collected enough water from the sloping shoulders of Rough Tor and Lower White Tor to call itself a brook, with a flow bubbling over peat-stained boulders which is wide and deep enough to attract the attention of Man. A weir, with concrete slope as slippery as the Devil himself partially dams the brook, and from this, with a sluice to control the water level, is bled off a quite remarkable tiny man-made canal known as the Devonport Leat. This leat was constructed in the late eighteenth century to bleed off a water supply for 'Dock'

as Devonport was then known, but at that time it did not start from this point.

Originally the leat was taken from the Blackbrook River, a lower tributary of West Dart which joins about one mile south of Two Bridges. It was in the late 1790s that the Company of Proprietors of Plymouth Dock Waterworks obtained rights to leat water from West Dart, and the first granite-lined channel was cut during 1793 and 1794. This ran for some 27 miles, following the contours of the hills and always gently sloping down as it went. A few years later the final six miles of this fascinating 33 mile long waterway was cut to augment the flow from this weir.

Considering that the leat was built some sixty years before Brunel's Saltash bridge was complete, it really is a quite outstanding piece of engineering and makes a fascinating course for an organised walk. If you start from the weir and keep to the leat with watery dedication you may be sure that, after one or two unexpected experiences, you will end up coming out of a pipe into Dousland Water Treatment Works some five miles southwest as the crow flies. The rest of it is now disused.

But back to West Dart. Half a mile below the weir from which that leat is bled, as you follow the stream southward toward its first small valley, you will see on the east bank what you might mistake for a scruffy copse of misshapen bushes, scarce worth a second glance. They seem to cling desperately to the lower slope of Longaford Tor solely by virtue of the fact that hereabouts there is a ragged outcrop of 'clitter'—boulders dislodged from the higher areas of the Tor and left lying at random near the valley floor most probably when the last ice-age receded. Ill-gotten it looks, this copse, and of little significance. How wrong can one be? This is Wistman's Wood, probably unique in that it is believed to be the highest surviving primeval oak grove in all Great Britain.

Eric Hemery in his classic book *Historic Dart* states that some of these gnarled trunks are probably five hundred years old. They are bowed by the fearsome northwest winds which sear down the valley, forced to send their branches downward rather than up since their tops rarely reach a height of fifteen feet before being shorn off by those winds. What little shelter they get is provided by Longaford

Left: The weir from which the leat is bled with Wistman's Wood in background. Below: Devonport leat follows the contours of the hills.

and Beardown Tors, and that the copse has survived at all is undoubtedly due to the litter of huge boulders which allow the seeds to lie in cracks, undisturbed by grazing stock and protected until firm roots are established.

How the wood got its rather odd name is uncertain but legend has it that the Druids, sometimes known as the 'Wise Men', considered Dartmoor one huge temple and held this spot in particularly high regard. It could well be that from the original 'Wise Men' has come the present 'Wistman'. At any rate, if one does not really know, it is as good an explanation as any other. The wood was all but lost entirely in 1886 when it caught fire. Methinks it must have been a ferociously hot, dry summer for one would more easily ignite the lichen on those rocks than the fungoid-infested wet boles of those contorted trees.

It is a weird and eerie place with a spirit of its own, alien to modern man, almost turning its back on the twentieth century as though lost in primordial memories of Earth as she was before we trod her face. You will be glad to get away before nightfall, for those grotesque boles mirror the fertile imagination of Arthur Rackham himself, invoking a weird and nightmare life into monstrous inanimate forms.

A notice adjacent, erected by the Nature Conservancy Council, emphasises the need for the public to be aware of its uniqueness and vulnerability, and alien though it may feel, we must respect this place for it is being closely studied and is yielding up much information about the types of flora and fauna originally existing on the Moor when a great deal of it was covered with such dense low forest.

When you are through the wood and have emerged back into the here-and-now, you may cast a glance behind and upstream to Rough Tor with its strangely isolated capstone up there on the horizon, while downstream you will make out the line of a crumbling dry stone wall with a stile. Make for this stile and sit here a while looking toward Two Bridges, for about half a mile distant and slightly to the left but just out of sight round the bluff of the hill is perhaps the most famous and historic Tor on Dartmoor. Not by any means the

Right: Wistman's Wood, invoking weird and nightmare life into monstrous inanimate forms.

most spectacular or the highest, it is best seen from the B3212 road to Postbridge just before you come to the Cherrybrook Hotel. This is the renowned Crockern Tor where, as far back as 1305, the famous Tinners' Assembly known as the Stannary Parliament used to meet.

Stannary means tin mine, and it was here under these great outcrops that the rules and general administration of mining in the area are said to have been thrashed out. Written records are in existence of the rulings made by that Parliament between the years 1494 and 1703. You walk on hallowed ground when exploring these heights, for you may be sure that strong emotions often accompanied the decisions, and many men's lives were profoundly influenced by a pronouncement made beneath these rocks. In those days Devon was divided into four Stannary Districts each with its own Stannary Town (tin market). Plympton, Tavistock, Chagford and Ashburton were the four towns chosen and the boundaries of all four Districts met here at Crockern Tor. Each District had twenty-four representatives known as jurats.

On selected dates all 96 of these representatives would assemble

Crumbling dry stone wall with a stile, looking back to Wistman's Wood.

18

Crockern Tor where the Stannary Parliament met.

here to disport themselves around the officiating 'chair', a granite boulder conveniently shaped, in front of which, if we are to believe our forbears, stood a large granite flat-topped 'table'. The President would be the Lord Warden of the Stannaries, an office held by some historic names among which are that of Sir Philip Champernowne in 1533 and Sir Walter Raleigh in 1600. Apparently a bluff of granite behind the 'chair' acted as a splendid sounding-board so that even in the winds which habitually blow up here, the assembled company could hear what was said.

The place was obviously chosen, in addition to the convenient acoustics, because it lay beside the old packhorse way, a track which spanned Dartmoor from Exeter to Tavistock. This track crossed West Dart at Two Bridges by means of a ford and clapper bridge, now gone.

Hemery, in *Historic Dart* says that the Judge's 'table' and 'chair', as they were known, were later removed some two and a half

The granite-slab at Dunnabridge farm. Was this the Stannary table from Crockern Tor?

miles east to Dunnabridge Pound. Rumour today has it that the 'table' top is at Dunnabridge Farm so I searched it out. As for the 'chair' it is said to be built into the wall close left of the farm gate into the Pound, but which of the stones now forming the granite 'settle' came from Crockern—if any— is a matter for conjecture. Certainly they had disappeared by 1795 for a Mr John Laskey when enquiring for their whereabouts, was told that they had been removed... not to Dunnabridge but to Prince Hall about a mile to the west of the Pound. William Crossing, probably the greatest authority on Dartmoor affairs, denies that the 'chair' was ever taken to the Pound. Wherever and for whatever purpose that chair and table were taken, it is certain that somebody must have wanted them very badly, or had an overpowering sense of history, for it would have taken a stout team of horses and much swearing to do the job!

Sitting here on the stile we can see, a mile downstream, the present Two Bridges where the merged B3212 and B3357 roads cross West Dart. Often it is assumed that the name 'Two Bridges' refers to the present modern road bridge and the seventeenth-century and very beautiful turnpike bridge close alongside. In fact the name is more likely to originate from the early sixteenth-century word *Tobrygge* which means 'at the bridge'.

Today, of course, the famous Two Bridges Hotel, a modernised eighteenth-century coaching inn, fulfils the pleasant task of speeding travellers on their way with added cheer. But should you stop here and happen to cast your eye across the meadows you might blink in disbelief, thinking that the 'cheer' had been a bit too liberal, for there, grazing contentedly on the coarse meadow grass, is a small herd of full-grown llamas!

Mr and Mrs Forbes-Wood, present proprietors of the hotel, brought these llamas from Bridport where at that time there was a herd of twenty or so. They keep five of them here simply as pets. Llamas in the natural habitat of Peru are shorn for their wool like sheep, but this small herd are spared that indignity and lead an indolent life, startled only by the occasional slightly apprehensive photographer who creeps up on them unaware. But they do lend a sort of Alice-in-Wonderland atmosphere to the river, so incongruous do they seem on the lonely Moor.

It is from here at Two Bridges where the Cowsic River augments the West Dart that the latter really begins to consider itself a true river. Incidentally, if your sojourn up here has saturated your appetite for bleak windswept skyscapes, deflect for a moment up this Cowsic River for half a mile or so: you will pass into lovely tree-shrouded glens which make a refreshing antidote for the eyes after the wild and barren world we have been wandering in. It may be that the junction with this small tributary does something to change the mind of West Dart regarding separate identity. At any rate it is from Two Bridges that the river appears to make the decision to fuse with its twin away there to the east.

One feels from this point that the river has a sense of purpose. It has gathered muscle, and begins to dictate a little to its environ, instead of being passively deflected wherever an inconvenient rock or hillock may lie in the way. Small boulders are piled up at odd corners... a sign that the water catchment area upstream has become large enough for the 'freshets'—sudden floods—to wreak occasional havoc.

21

The river is beginning to impose its character on the locality, and the eye is rarely unaware of it when scanning the scene. Perhaps that is why the Devon Local Education Authority chose a point just over a mile downstream from the road bridge, to build the Dartmoor Training Centre. The track to this Centre comes via a magnificent tree-lined colonnade from the B3357 where a sign for the Prince Hall Hotel now catches the eye. This track passes close by the hotel and continues on to span the river by a lovely old hump-back single arch stone bridge before carrying on to Moorlands Farm. The modern purpose-built Centre lies close by the bridge and has been provided for use by schools and youth groups. A very worthwhile enterprise it is, for it has given untold numbers of youngsters under adult supervision probably their first taste of real freedom in the countryside coupled with a sense of responsibility for themselves and the environ they are enjoying. Beautifully situated in Dartmoor National Park, it is ideally suited for residential work or conferences, field studies and indeed any outdoor pursuits and organised courses.

The land which abuts the Centre is, of course, privately owned. Please note that there is no public right-of-way along the river here, either upstream or down. Full details of rights-of-way and the names of landowners in the area is given in the Centre's informative 'Users' Handbook', which is available from the Chief Education Officer, County Hall, Exeter EX2 4QG to whom any enquiries should be made.

Standing full-face toward the river and some two hundred yards from its north bank, almost within sight of the Centre, is Prince Hall Hotel, an eyecatching Georgian mansion whose resident proprietors are Mr and Mrs P.R. Harrison. This nine-bedroomed hotel is lovingly cared for and run by these two self-confessed 'Dartmoorphiles' and it was with delight that Mr Harrison gave me a succinct history of the place. 'The house was built in 1787 for Sir Francis Buller,' he told me as we sat in the spacious lounge looking over the lawns and fields stretching down to the river. 'Buller was an interesting character because at the age of 32 he was the youngest person ever to be made a High Court Judge in this

A llama . . . startled by a slightly apprehensive photographer.

country. He died in 1800 and the house was then taken over by a family called Gullett who lived here for six years after which, if local knowledge is to be relied on, the place was used as an annexe to the prison which, as you know, lies two and a half miles west as the crow flies.

'I'm fairly sure that during that time the place housed several very senior French prisoners of war together with their servants. By the end of that war, in 1815, Mr Gullett had died and the Fowlers took over with a concept of farming the land and growing vegetables on a fairly large scale. This proved to be a failure, and so far as I can gather the only root vegetable they managed to produce in quantity was the turnip! At this time there were 2,600 odd acres attached to the place, so they had every opportunity to produce in bulk. After the Fowlers came the Lambs who, ironically, were responsible for first introducing the black-faced sheep onto Dartmoor, and later the Galloway cattle.

'Around 1866 the house was taken over by the Barringtons—he was Steward for the Duchy of Cornwall—and they lived here until 1906 after which there is a blank in the records for six years when in 1912 the Pethericks came and opened it as an hotel. It may well be that during those previous six years they used it as a private house. Be that as it may I know that when they opened the place for residents the price per head per week was three pounds for full board!

'The place closed down during the war years but opened again in 1918 until 1922 when the Petherick family, having become fairly ancient, lost interest in the commerical side of things. In 1923 the place was bought by a family called Alder who turned out to be somewhat ill-fated, for the father was killed by being pitched head-first through the window here from his horse, and the son tragically drowned while swimming down in the river. By 1931 the house was in sad disrepair and during a very heavy fall of snow in that year the roof collapsed.

'Now rumour has it that shortly afterwards King Edward VIII came here with Mrs Simpson. In fact, this is not strictly true for he stayed at Tor Royal near Princetown and kept his horses here in a stable at the back—some 48 horses—and also held garden parties among the dahlia beds for which the place was noted... you may still see the slight rise out there where the beds were sited under the copper beech tree.

24

West Dart from the road near Dunnabridge Pound.

'In 1936 the house was bought by a Captain Llewellyn who came here with his wife and five small children, living in some style and refurbishing the place into something of its former glory. There is a rather pleasing story told of the Captain. Apparently one day nearby he saw some people throwing litter onto the Moor beside the road. He took their car number as they drove off when he tried to take them to task, and by this means traced them to Yorkshire. He then packed all the litter into two large tea-chests with a bit of granite for good measure and sent it to them—cash on delivery! The enclosed note simply said: "You left something behind."

'A man dear to my heart,' he chuckled, 'for I do loathe litterbugs. Well, Captain Llewellyn was called up in 1940 and never came back to the place, but in 1945 Lord and Lady Astor came here and stayed for eleven months—this room was their billiard room—and later they let it as a retreat for the deprived children of Plymouth. Then the property was bought by a Dr Bentley, the prison doctor, who lived here more or less as a recluse for some 22 years, using I understand only two rooms.'

'And how', I asked, 'did you find the place?'

'Wandering across the Moor one day my wife and I simply fell in

25

Prince Hall bridge below the Training Centre.

love with it. It was in an appalling state of disrepair so we had to set about renovating it. New ceilings, floors, windows—and we installed central heating. We did extensive alterations, keeping wherever possible to the original style. There is so much potential here in a magnificent setting, and we are working daily on refurbishing the gardens and outbuildings. We have our own electricity supply of course from two generators.

'By the way,' said Peter Harrison as I got into my car to leave, 'apparently the "Prince" of Prince Hall has nothing to do with Princetown over there. Originally it was spelt "Prynse" and the bridge spanning the river down there is on record in about 1740 as being "Prynse Hall Bridge". There are records of this house going back to 1434.'

Yes, I mused as I drove back along the lovely quarter-mile long colonnade of elegant beech trees, they did know how to site houses in those days and there are centuries of history sleeping in that place. Good to know that it has once more fallen into caring hands: and what a magnificent spot for a holiday!

* * * * * *

The river continues making its way eastward while getting to know yet more new water from Blackbrook which sweeps in from the west, and Cherrybrook from the north, obviously enjoying the experience for it is fairly bowling along from recent rain farther up in the hills. At a set of ancient stepping stones, only just visible under the torrent it swings northeast as though keen to renew acquaintance with the Two Bridges-Dartmeet road close by Dunnabridge farm. But a rapid change of mind occurs when it sights the road far above on the steep hillside. Motorists may, with little effort, get a splendid 'birds' eye' view of the Dart's silvered course from just east of Dunnabridge Pound.

The Pound, which is almost circular and encloses an area larger than some of the small fields hereabouts, is best seen from the air. To an inexperienced eye at ground level the curving sweep of its dry stone walls might easily be mistaken for a regular field 'hedge'. Long ago, stock belonging to unlicensed owners, if found grazing in Dartmoor Forest to the north, was herded annually into this Pound by those with privileged pasturage, and by the peat-cutters. It was one of the duties the latter performed in return for such privileges and it must have been a noisy and lively event, for wild moorland ponies do not willingly submit to loss of freedom.

Below the Pound the river is now flowing through an intricate pattern of medieval settlements. Indeed the small fields we see along her banks form what is probably the oldest pattern of still worked farmland in Britain. In turn the ancient tenement lands of Prince Hall, Broom Park, Dunnabridge, Brownberry, Sherberton, Hexworthy and Huccaby are all drained thereby, and it is just north of Sherberton that the River Swincombe sweeps up to join West Dart from the south, augmenting it with water drained from the long since disused tin mining area at Whiteworks, weaving in around the foot of Ter Hill and Down Ridge.

West Dart flows under the road to Hexworthy, spanned by a splendid twin-arched bridge built at the end of the eighteenth-century when the original clapper bridge was washed away with the loss of a man's life. When storms pour their contents onto the high peaks of the Moor these rivers naturally increase their volume many times and a surge or 'freshet' of frightening power can bowl headlong down the valleys, sweeping really large rocks along like battering-rams. Often the onslaught is powerful enough to lift enormous slabs of granite, carrying them hundreds of yards downstream. Such was the case here, and there is now no sign of the original clapper bridge; its components are probably long since buried deep somewhere under the riverbed. A very ancient track from Huccaby Farm to Combestone Tor crosses the river at Week Ford before the latter again swings northeast into a deepening valley which is thickly clothed with trees.

If you listen now, standing a little back from the bank so as to soften the river's voice, you may under certain conditions hear a far-off answering call of running water. It is East Dart, full of its own importance for it is slightly more full-grown than this, its twin, flowing and chattering ever closer under the steep slopes of Yar Tor ahead. Very soon they will fuse and move into another and quite different phase of being, for they are falling down to a level where conifers do not feel so much at home... where the more indigenous broadleaved woods flank deeper valleys and speak of a more protected lush environ.

Dartmeet is the place of their union and change. But first East Dart has her own story to tell.

II
East Dart

But I know that in you a spirit doth live
And a word in you this day.

Charles Kingsley

We are back with the sky again close by Whitehorse Hill high on the Moor above all Devon, and that sky is rinsed a clear blue after recent rain. The clouds—just the snow-white flank of them low down Chagford way—are receding fast before a spanking west wind that sets the blood tingling.

Often at sea, as a sailor in my chosen environ of water and sky, I've wished to take wing like a bird and soar over the waves. Up here, why, one is already halfway to Heaven. It is a truly glorious place where one's spirit may fly free as that wind and I would gladly slough off the sheer limitation that gravity imposes on this dense body. There is the tang of heath and heather in the air, and that indescribable scent of wet peaty grasses one comes across in the Highlands of Scotland.

Within the circle of my horizon the marshes drain away to form, in all, the beginnings of seven rivers, and we are even farther into the heart of the Moor than the source of West Dart, for this East Dart rises close under Hangingstone Hill a mere few hundred yards from where the Taw starts its flow northward to the Bristol Channel. The East Dart flows almost due south for a mile or so before being joined by Cut Hill stream coming in from the west, whence the course deflects slightly to the east into Broad Marsh and Sandy Hole Pass—the latter a miniature boulderstrewn gorge at the foot of Winney's Down.

You would think none had ever lived so far away from human

29

The ruin of Statts House, home of a peat cutter.

companionship and any contact with society and its comforts, but if
you climb the southeast side of Winney's Down you will come
across a small ruin. It is Statts House, home of a peat cutter who
made a livelihood here around the mid-eighteenth century. It was
about that time that the cutting of peat on the loneliest parts of the
Moor commenced, due to an increasing demand from the mines and
from the fast expanding towns farther down on the fringes of
Dartmoor. It must have been a bleak occupation, calling for an
unusual disposition in a man, or maybe it was simply a matter of
sheer survival.

Be that as it may, you will come across one or two of these small
granite hovels in these marshy areas. They measure little more than
twelve feet by seven overall, and Statts House is one of them, a
mere ruin now, but we know that the doorway was very low and
narrow so that the occupant had to crawl in on all fours—a small
price to pay for the greater warmth inside. Both ends of this house
were rounded, and in one of them you may see traces of a cupboard
recess with a small fireplace nearby. The peat was cut in springtime
and stacked in layers called 'stooks' to dry, after which it was

carried by packhorse before the advent of autumn rains down to wherever the best price could be obtained.

We modern folk may well wonder at the life of its solitary occupant, cooped in here at night while the winds seared over and between the peaks all round. No radio then, nor television, and probably unable to read what few books were available, such a life must have led to profound introspection and probably fairly narrow interests.

Yet even the legendary Statt probably had some human contact, for as the stream of East Dart weaves away on the first mile or so of its 1,840 foot drop to the sea, and the peat becomes slightly less predominant, you will find yourself picking your way between and over what are obviously unnatural heaps of spoil. They have been dug out from either side of the stream and an immense amount of labour has been expended in so doing. But wherever there is money to be made you will find Man hell-bent on making as much of it as he possibly can, and if the environ suffers in the process. . .well, what of it?

Of course this is the philosophy of an effete twentieth-century mortal living in a society which has organised technology to take the hard edge off survival and I might have had a different attitude had I lived in those days when the open-cast tin mining flourished.

Often, they diverted the streams and rivers by means of artificial trenches in order to drain off the area they wanted to comb. Enormous amounts of waste silt and gravel resulted, and the clever idea of getting rid of some of it by causing an artificial bottleneck in an embryonic East Dart just downstream at Sandy Hole Pass was hit upon. It is much easier to pour waste into a fast-flowing stream which will sweep it down and away from your working area than it is to haul it off by horsedrawn carts!

The ruse worked splendidly so far as the tinners were concerned, and East Dart became an effective waste-disposal scheme. But, as is often the case, 'one man's meat is another man's poison'. The scheme worked altogether too well, and, incredible though it may seem, after a few years those in control of the harbour at Dartmouth some 45 miles away made a complaint in Parliament that the harbour was suffering from a build-up of deposits from, and pollution by, this tinners' waste!

Strong in complaint was one Sir Richard Strode, MP for Plympton, and it is an indication of the power of the Stannary

Parliament up there on Crockern Tor that they promptly took Strode to task, imposing a very large fine of £160 for trying to interfere with the rights of the tinners. He ignored the fine and was summarily seized by Stannary officers and thrown into the notorious Lydford Castle prison. But the tinners had bitten off rather more than they could chew, and eventually King Henry VIII—never a man to cross lightly—personally intervened. He ordered the immediate release of Strode and further decreed, in 1533, that the tinners cease using the river for that purpose, and that they carry the waste instead to a place from which there was no chance of it being washed down, even when in full flood. History lessons have not left me with a high regard for that particular king, but on this score I'm wholly with him. The order applied to all tinners on the Moor, and was a salutary chastening of what looked bent on becoming a rather tyrannous body.

Just south of Sandy Hole Pass the granite strata protrudes from under the bed of the river to form a low but quite beautiful little

The waterfall just south of Sandy Hole Pass.

Sandy Hole Pass below Broad Marsh.

waterfall. The stream tumbles over the edge of a granite shelf some eight feet into a little pool served by a naturally moulded seat of granite. You may sit and dabble hot feet into the cascade, or stand and let the ice-cold flow completely engulf you, then dry off on the massive flat slabs close by. You will get a tan here quicker than down at sea-level, for 1,800 feet less atmosphere makes a significant difference to the strength of the sun's rays. It is a wonderful place for a picnic on a summer afternoon if you are moderately fit and wish to blow all the cares of the world away.

We are now about two and a half miles from Postbridge as the river wiggles, and it is not the easiest of walking so you should take care not to be caught by sundown and darkness. Always carry a compass if you come this far onto the Moor, and a useful tip, if you do decide to leave the stream and set off onto the largely featureless grassy downs... take careful note of how you are walking in relation to the wind direction. If visibility closes in, or you lose your compass, it is a rough indication of a reciprocal direction which will bring you back to the stream, from whence you may pick your way with the current back to recognisable points and civilisation.

From the waterfall the stream sweeps in a small bow northward to be joined by Winney Down stream and others before looping back southward for a mile and a half to pass under the road at Postbridge. A lovely three-arched bridge spans the river here, close alongside a magnificent and intact clapper bridge dating from the thirteenth century. It is worth studying, not only to marvel at the tensile strength of granite manifest in the long horizontal 'imposts', but to wonder just how men, without the aid of cranes or bulldozers, managed to lift the enormous lintels into place.

Postbridge is some three and a half miles east of Two Bridges on the B3212 and it is in this area that interesting archaeological finds have been unearthed in the form of flint arrowheads, knives and scrapers for cleaning hides. Our Mesolithic ancestors some ten thousand years ago used these but the fascinating fact is that flint is not found naturally in granite areas: it had to be brought from the chalklands of west Dorset and east Devon. The artifacts found hereabout are now exhibited in the Royal Albert Museum at Exeter.

South of the road, and clothing much of the west bank of the river is the first large area of real trees. These are conifers, set as a plantation after the last war and looking somewhat incongruous in this environ, to which they are anything but natural. But they do provide some work for the inhabitants of Bellever, a little colony of houses about one mile south of Postbridge, and the forest also provides much needed timber.

* * * * * *

There is another fine three-arched bridge at Bellever, built soon after the Napoleonic wars, which carries the small unclassified road across. As at Postbridge it has an older clapper bridge close alongside, but some of the 'imposts'—the horizontal slabs—are missing. Their whereabouts are unknown but it is quite possible that by virtue of their length and thickness they were split

Postbridge with the fine original clapper bridge alongside.

longitudinally for gateposts after the later bridge was completed. If you walk downstream on the grassy east bank, in less than one mile you will come across a small copse of conifers which looks as though it had spilled across the river from the forest. About 300 yards into this copse, some 100 feet or so from the riverbank and quite engulfed by the trees is Whiteslade Farm, or rather the crumbling ruins of it, nicknamed Snaily House on account of a weird but rather sad story.

The river here runs into a deep high-sided valley originally known as Lough Tor Hole, and in this farmhouse on its bank over a century ago lived two spinster sisters. Solitary, and without visible means of support, they became in their later years something of a mystery for they were seldom if ever seen at nearby Postbridge or Babeny. They spent no money on food and appeared to survive on thin air. Rumour had it that they ate grass, for they kept no stock of any sort. Gradually more serious rumour began circulating, as tends to happen when idle minds have nothing better to do but speculate. Was there Witchcraft afoot? Eventually local curiosity and

**Ruin of 'Snaily House'.
Note the doorway behind
the fallen tree.**

suspicion became so intense that an organised group of half-fearful,
half-angry locals marched to the house where, despite the obvious
perplexity and demeanour of the two inhabitants, they searched the
place for signs of evildoing. They found nothing by way of grounded
broomsticks or 'familiars' in the form of enigmatic black cats... nor
yet did they find any recognisable food. Yet the two old women were
obviously in good health and it was only when by chance the lid was
removed from a large iron pot that the situation became clear: it was
filled with juicy garden snails, pickled into a jelly!

From that day on, so the story goes, the two sisters pined away.
Perhaps the revulsion shown by the intruders shamed them, or even
took away their appetite for what was evidently their staple diet.
Whatever the cause, it is said that from that day on they gradually
declined in health and eventually were found dead. Hence the name
'Snaily House' lives on, today nothing but a miserable dank ruin
among the pines, green with moss and overgrown with brambles.
You may still make out a walled pathway up the steep valley side of
Riddon Ridge which once gave access to the house, though I

imagine as the two old folk got on in years they might have preferred the level, if longer, route to Bellever should they ever have felt like company.

* * * * * *

Donny did not wish to be photographed!

Why should he stare at the alarming Cyclopean glass eye in the middle of this stranger's forehead? Much better to seek the security of Ruth Murray's warm and comforting neck. Which he did despite my ineffective badger noises—and what sort of noise does a badger make, anyway? 'Certainly not *that*,' called Ruth. 'You'll frighten him to death!' She struggled to keep the forty pound bundle of cuddly wriggling fur happy until one blissful moment when *Donny* coyly half-looked at me. You see the result.

Snug among the pines of the Forestry Commission's plantation on the sloping west bank of Lough Tor Hole, and almost opposite the sad remains of 'Snaily House' is Mrs Ruth Murray's Field Study Centre at Laughter Hole farm. The name undoubtedly derives from the original Lough Tor (Laughter Tor) which lies close westward. You reach the Centre by a private gated track and by appointment only, for Mrs Murray tolerates casual callers ill. This is not surprising for, since her husband died the days do not seem to have held enough hours in which to run this active Centre which embraces what has become known as the badger sanctuary. She was busy tending some sixty of these delightful mammals when I persuaded her to give me an interview. Most of them had been brought to her as a result of severe wounding at the hands of Man, either by accident or deliberately.

The Centre and Ruth Murray have become internationally famous since she worked in close liaison with the Earl of Arran to draft the 1973 Badger Protection Act which makes it illegal to dig out or bait the badger, and I asked her to talk about this interesting and really worthwhile enterprise.

'My husband and I did not start this place as a badger sanctuary,' she told me. 'Originally we farmed at Thorndon near Okehampton and, having a natural interest in wild life, we set up a small Field Study Centre there, calling it exactly that. Interest in the Centre increased locally, and when we retired from farming in the late 1960s and eventually bought this place we brought some of the animals with us, such as my bloodhounds and a few badgers we were nursing at the time.

'Like Topsy, the place has just grown since then. Children bring me specimens and the local schools arrange visits, so more and more people have come to know of the place and, of course, my own knowledge and expertise has increased. In turn the vets working with me have become more knowledgeable, particularly about badgers which, poor creatures, have across the whole history of Man seemed to attract his wrath and cruelty. "Badger Baiting" has been a "sport" for centuries and the sad thing is that one of the reasons for this is the quite incredible courage of the creature. Even though torn badly by the dogs which are set upon them and hacked by the spades of the brutes who pin them in their setts so that the dogs can have their sport, they will continue to defend themselves to their last breath. So they put on a "good show" for those with a taste for that sort of thing.

'The numbers I nurse here do fluctuate of course,' she added. 'Obviously one is releasing some as they become fit to return to life in the wild. I would like to release more than I do, but I have certain restrictions placed on me by the Ministry of Agriculture. Badgers are not allowed to be translocated—shifted from one area to another—because of the idea that they spread tuberculosis.

'Badgers are quite harmless if left alone,' Ruth continued, 'but one characteristic of theirs can make them react quite violently. You see, there is a public misconception that they have poor eyesight. This is not the case; they have quite average eyesight, about as good as a dog, but they have a very highly developed sense of smell and therefore work primarily with this sense. The result is that sometimes when a badger is "on a scent" it may approach a person very close, concentrating totally on the scent of whatever it may be following, until its other sense—that of sight— "switches on" as it were. It will then sheer away violently, which may be taken as aggression. In a fashion we humans are much the same, but in the reverse way: we work primarily on the sense of sight. This does not mean that we have no sense, or even a poor sense, of smell. It is just that we choose not to use it as our prime "window" on the outside world. So, as I say, a badger can on occasion walk right up to one. . . before getting your scent, when they will sheer off quickly. Their sense of smell is incredible, better I suspect than that of the bloodhound, and they use it to find food, avoid danger, and mark

Donny did not wish to be photographed!

their territory. For the latter purpose they have a scent gland under their tails, and leave their scent by simply sitting down. It's a sign of friendliness if one sits on my toes—he or she is marking me as being acceptable within their territory.'

Male badgers are called boars, the females sows, probably on account of their habit of grubbing about rather like a pig and grunting while searching for the small insects and rodents which form their main diet. They have become largely nocturnal as a result of their fear of Man, and they do not hibernate in winter as is often thought: one may follow their distinctive five-toed footprints across

Dartmeet. The boulders in East Dart make splendid islands for children to play on.

snow in midwinter. A fully developed male adult can measure over three feet in length, and the burrows, or setts as they are called, are generally made in soft ground such as chalk or sandy soil, or in the cracks between rocks. They are found in all our counties and are very clean, home-loving animals. Setts may extend for as much as one hundred yards underground with enlarged chambers dotted along them. They use these to sleep in, on a dried bed of bracken or moss which they periodically bring out, using the two forepaws and chin to hold it while shuffling backwards. After leaving it in the sun and wind for an airing they take it back down below. Whole generations of badgers will live in one large sett and they seem to carry a blueprint in their minds of the layout, because if the sett is destroyed for any reason they will reconstruct an identical copy in the same area.

'*Donny*', said Ruth, 'was found lying on a cart track in a deep coma in Somerset, his sister beside him dead. The two young cubs had been thrown aside after their sett had been dug out and the adults killed. His two companions in the same pen are also cubs born this spring. One of them came from north Devon and we call him *Arvon* after the Arvon Foundation on whose land his sett was built. They are very proud to have badgers on their land, but he was found lying in a sorry state on the verge of a track with severe dog bites on his throat and ear. Normally a dog will not attack a badger; it generally means that men are involved for they have to train the dogs to "bait" them. Now, thankfully, it is illegal to sell badger pelts but, being the sort of men they are, if they come across one in a defenceless state they will set their dogs on it just for fun. You should not try to handle one,' she cautioned, 'unless you have previously made friends for, quite naturally, they look upon Man as one of their worst enemies, and they have a tenacious bite.'

I left the Centre with a feeling of deep respect for this lady who is quite devoid of unrealistic sentimentality. She is simply concerned with alleviating the suffering of what is, after all, a very attractive and lovable creature. May such Field Study Centres spread throughout our land, divorced as we steadily become from any sense of responsibility for, or dependency on, our environ and its wild life.

* * * * * *

From Laughter Hole the river sweeps south of Babeny where a very ancient track, now a public footpath, crosses it by a few remaining stepping stones known as Babeny Steps. A clapper bridge once spanned the flow here, but this was carried away long since by one of those disastrous 'freshets'. The track, which is an extension of that leading past Laughter Hole Farm, after passing through Babeny and crossing the river, follows the west bank through woods then climbs up to the ancient tenement of Brimpts Farm where, in the season, you may rest for a very enjoyable hour while relishing a farmhouse cream tea. From the farm it continues on to join the B3357 road near the junction to Hexworthy.

We are approaching now what is perhaps one of the best known and loved areas of the river: Badgers Holt and Dartmeet. This meeting place annually greets some quarter of a million visitors and it is not difficult to see why this should be the case. Two rivers meet, which itself is of picturesque interest. There is a spacious car park with every facility attending and it lies off the B3357 from

Paul Way, proprietor of Badgers Holt, with
wildlife in background.

Tavistock to Ashburton so that access is very easy. There is the
ruin of an old clapper bridge which children—and adults—may
clamber over, and great rounded boulders strew the shallow East
Dart just upstream which make enchanted islands for the
youngsters to take possession of and hold against enemy invaders,
or fall off and ruin holiday clothes while father snoozes after lunch
on the wide grassy banks.

Some two hundred yards upstream from the car park along a well-
paved path is the Badgers Holt licensed restaurant. The proprietor
Paul Way, with his large staff, quite obviously enjoys acting as host

to a constant stream of hungry and thirsty visitors, and I can personally vouch for the value of what he supplies, for where else in 1986 may you eat your way through a three course menu, with a choice of each course, plus coffee, for around £4? Close alongside the restaurant, which used to be a fishing lodge, is a small wildlife sanctuary... well, the life is wild in large cages rather like an open-air aviary, although you may well find yourself sharing your biscuits with a magnificent peacock or two which roam freely about and fly up to the rooftops just to keep a regal eye on things.

The Way family are not newcomers to this county, and it was while having my lunch there and chatting with Paul that I spied, screwed to the wall, a magnificent etching of Dartmoor Harbour in the days of sailing ships. Seagull's-eye-view it is, for they didn't have helicopters in those days. 'The artist was a great, great . . . or maybe even great, great, great uncle of mine,' grinned Paul as I unscrewed the picture to photograph it in sunlight (page 103), dodging meanwhile the elbows of browsers enjoying themselves in the gift and bookshop adjacent to the restaurant. It is a vital place, fit for the banks of one of the loveliest rivers in all Devon.

We are in the Manor of Spitchwick now, mentioned in the Domesday Book, and Brimpts Wood opposite the Badgers Holt, while being in the county of Devon, does in fact form part of the Duchy of Cornwall. County Bridge which carries the present road across the river just north of the junction with West Dart was built in 1792 and some may say it is a great pity it was not built just that little bit wider, for it can be tricky meeting a fifty-seater coach thereon. But there is succour to hand, for you may always take your buckled vehicle into the car park and seek solace at the Holt!

The 'twins' are no more. They have joined forces into what is known locally as the Double Dart, and together with yet greater strength they plunge straight into an ever-deepening wooded valley which has a totally different atmosphere from anything we have yet experienced on our wanderings down from the high Moor.

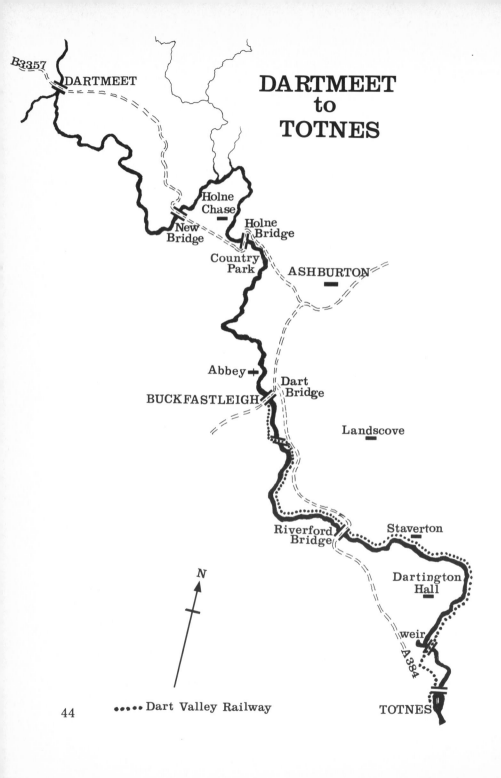

B3357
DARTMEET

DARTMEET
to
TOTNES

Holne
Chase
New   Holne
Bridge   Bridge

Country
Park

ASHBURTON

Abbey
BUCKFASTLEIGH   Dart
                     Bridge

Landscove

Riverford   Staverton
Bridge

Dartington
Hall

N

weir

A384

44   •••• Dart Valley Railway   TOTNES

III
Dartmeet to Dartington

I cannot tell what you say, green leaves,
I cannot tell what you say;
But I know that there is a spirit in you
And a word in you this day.

Charles Kingsley

We know that, back in 1240, the two rivers upstream of Dartmeet were called *Derta* and *Aliam Derta*—the latter meaning 'another Dart'. By the early 1600s they were being referred to as 'Easter' and 'Wester' Dart and the actual name Dartmeet was first recorded in 1616.

Certainly the next ten miles or so of the Dart is, for my money, the most beautiful stretch for it now begins to enter what might be called a state of young maturity. There is a new strength in the flow now, indeed the missing parts of the clapper bridge at Dartmeet were swept away in a 'freshet' of 1826—and that was water from East Dart alone!

Walk downstream from Dartmeet and you will be entering what is sometimes called the border country of Dartmoor. It is a belt of quite characteristic countryside fringing the Moor and spanning that area between the bleak uplands and the more populous lowland. This fringe is roughly three miles in width—somewhat more on the northeastern edge—and forms a sort of 'penumbra of transition' between the two levels. Within its confines the rivers pass through picturesque gorges, thickly wooded on the slopes with trees more representative of the English countryside, and at the outer limits of the fringe there is an altogether more pastoral feeling about it. Immediately south of Dartmeet the river plunges into the steepening valley of Combestone Wood, thence through almost continually tree-shrouded valleys past New Bridge, Holne Chase,

45

Dartmeet. East and West Dart join to form the magical river.

Southpark and Hembury Woods to finally cross the boundary of Dartmoor National Park just south of Buckfast.

If you wish to shake off the traumas of twentieth-century living and rid yourself for a day of that frenetic state of mind which is often engendered by our modern way of life, leave your car at Dartmeet and take the footpath on the east bank of the river. As you probe farther from the road you will find any company you may have had becomes thinner, and the path is not always easy of access, but you will enter a world of pure enchantment. To see it at its best go on a spring or autumn morning when the sunlight is glancing down through the trees to reflect off the water. Take care not to disturb the odd fisherman and silently follow the path alongside the river. Silently, I emphasise, for you are entering wonderland, and magic is easily dispelled.

There is something conducive to happiness and a relaxed sense of wellbeing when one spends an hour or so close to running water, most particularly if the stream or river be contained within a valley or gorge. T. Lethbridge, in his book *Ghost and Divining Rod*, makes some interesting observations on this fact, and many ancient teachings note the value to the human psyche of running water and waterfalls. If that water be fresh and clean from the high Moors, as this is, and lately enriched by glades where tree roots and other foliage add an almost herbal spice to it, then so much the better.

I give you here a recipe for enchantment! Lie on any one of the rounded boulders on Dart's bank. Choose a spot where the warming sun will bathe you and switch off the urgency of your thoughts: let them flit in and out of your mind like the butterflies they are, so that you may simply listen to nature. It casts a spell, the distant chuckle of flowing water coupled perhaps with the nearer, more specific bubbling laughter of some small cascade. From above you comes a scarce audible breath of air through trees up the valley side, and gradually it will almost seem that the water is flowing through you to carry away all tension, all dis-ease, stress and worry. Something deep within you starts to resonate in harmony with the pattern of nature all about. Things fall into proper perspective. It is more than just a rest: it is regeneration, and you will come away energised, as though you had been a battery on a trickle-charge, ready to face the problems that yesterday seemed all but insurmountable.

I tell you it is a delight, this valley from Dartmeet down to New Bridge. One mile downstream from Dartmeet on the north bank you will come across a small but powerful atmospheric combe with a stream trickling into the river. This is Warren House Pit, named after two Dartmoor warreners, Richard Reynell and Walter Furseland, who back in the 1600s established a rabbit-breeding business. Remember in those days rabbit meat was a very acceptable dish for the poorer members of society, and the two men in addition built ingenious vermin traps to catch the predators which nightly took off some of the cultivated rabbits. These consisted of small granite tunnels with funnelling walls which directed the vermin into the traps, though the exact nature of the trap itself I have been unable to discover. The Normans introduced rabbits to this country in 1066 and gradually the demand for their meat increased, so these commercial warrens spread throughout England. The first one recorded on the Moor was at Trowlesworthy on the River Plym, and this was still functioning in the mid 1900s.

A little farther down river is another similar valley running in from the north and directing the stream of Simons Lake into the river. Close by is an area known as Broadstone, originally Broada Stone, where the shape of the river bed can, under certain conditions combined with the required amount of water, apparently produce an unholy moaning known as the 'cry of the Dart'. I have sat here, not always in the best of weather, hoping to catch a spinechilling echo of it, but have to admit defeat.

The river continues down the steep valley to pass through Bellpool and Holne Woods on the west bank, all of which are National Trust property, and then swings north round Deadman's Corner and Lower Hannaford emerging via a thick bracken clad flatland to pass beneath the road again at New Bridge. This is almost as popular for picnicking as Dartmeet, and in season the staff on duty at the National Park office in the caravan on the car park, will supply any information you may require, and give you the current issue of *Dartmoor Visitor*, a newspaper issued by the National Park Authority and full of useful information and tips.

Below: Mary and Kenneth Bromage, proprietors of the Holne Chase Hotel. Right: Holne Chase Hotel . . . sanctuary from the ubiquitous god Car.

The river is running almost due north under this picturesque medieval bridge, and now enters another thickly wooded area on either bank at Chase Wood, Greypark Wood, and Ausewell Wood, sweeping as it does so in a wide arc north of the well-known Holne Chase hotel. Most of the banks here are private property with protected fishing rights, and permission is needed before members of the public may wander at will. However, for residents of the hotel about one mile of the west bank is accessible and the hotel owns the fishing rights of this stretch. Holne Chase itself was a hunting estate of the eleventh century, and the word *holne* comes from the old Saxon *holen* meaning holly, of which there is much hereabouts. Chase means hunting ground, and this area was exactly that for use of the pre-Reformation Abbots of Buckfast a little farther down river. The house around which the present buildings have been developed dates back to 1710, but much of the present frontage was added around 1832.

The house has been run as an hotel since 1934, but it was in 1972 that the present proprietors, Mary and Kenneth Bromage, took over the lease. Certainly you will go a long way before finding two

Far left: Members of Sherborne School canoeing club leave Holne bridge on an instructional trip, bound for Staverton. Left: John Hughes, Junior Parachute Company, Pirbright, Surrey, jumps from Holne bridge during his adventure training course.

more caring hosts, more homely and tasteful comfort, and anything to match the first-class cuisine. With fifteen rooms in all the hotel is small enough to cater for the individual needs of guests, and is far enough away from the main road to allow that sense of peace and tranquillity which is becoming more and more rare since we started worshipping the powerful and ubiquitous god *Car*.

One mile east as the crow flies from New Bridge the river, having completed its arc northwards round the Chase, is crossed by Holne Bridge, probably one of the most beautiful on the whole river. The original bridge was swept away in a flood, and the one we see today replaced it on the orders of Bishop Stafford of Exeter. It has three semi-circular arches and one segmental, an indulgence being granted by the Bishop to all who helped in the construction: a cheap and effective way the Church had in those times for playing on the conscience of a guilt-ridden populace to expedite such works.

The bridge is a favourite spot for canoeists who, having obtained the necessary permission depending upon the season, like to practice 'white water' work when the river is in flood. It makes exciting watching as they sweep beneath the bridge, negotiating all

Above: The beauty of the Dart near Holne bridge.
Right: Assault course in River Dart Country Park.

the boulders and whirlpool traps with commendable skill. Afterwards, if they feel like getting rid of excess energy—and they often do—you may catch them mounting the bridge parapet to jump the 25 feet or so into a conveniently deep pool beneath. All of this takes a great deal of spirit and results sometimes in much hooting of car horns when a motorist stops on the bridge, agape in disbelief!

South of Ausewell Wood the river makes another of its characteristic sweeps. North and east banks now border on meadows, but the opposite bank fronts the River Dart Country Park which provides practically all a family can possibly require for an enjoyable holiday, including pony-trekking, swimming in an outdoor pool, Tarzan-like activities with ropes, houses built in trees and a large camping area. This latter is adjacent to excavated lakes fed with water from the river, and there is a magnificent river-walk under mature beech trees where an army assault-course is laid out, definitely *not* for use by the visitors, though it is still used for training under supervision of the Centre's staff and makes one dizzy just to contemplate.

**Holne Park House, nucleus of the River Dart
Country Park and Residential Centre which provides
practically all that a family can require for an
enjoyable holiday.**

It is in the grounds of this Country Park that the eighth
bridge—counted from the two sources—spans the Dart. Known
locally as the 'Waterworks Bridge' it was constructed by Paignton
Urban District Council in 1904 to carry their water mains from
Venford Reservoir on the Moor to the Paignton area. Today it
carries the main access road to the Country Park and is probably
the 'youngest' bridge to span the river. For all its modernity it in no
way disfigures or appears out of keeping with this very beautiful
stretch of water.

The Residential Centre which forms the nucleus of the Country
Park is sited in a 100 roomed house standing in quite wonderful
gardens. During the last war this house was taken over by the RAF
as the Westcountry Signals Headquarters, having prior to that been
an hotel for a number of years. After the war it reverted to being an
hotel until the Outward Bound School took over tenancy for some
sixteen years prior to 1975 when the owners, Patrick and Carole
Simpson, decided to restore the estate to its former glory, the
grounds having been allowed to deteriorate. The Countryside
Commission helped in the restoration of the grounds, and the entire

54

park, which includes a restaurant and shop plus tennis and volley-ball courts, is open to residents and day visitors.

There is a subtle change taking place in the environs now: the east bank is becoming more pastoral and there are small but lush meadows opposite Hembury Wood which conceals, some four hundred feet above the river, the iron-age hilltop fort known as Hembury Castle. We are close to the border of the National Park, and there beside the river ahead is the tower of Buckfast Abbey, just showing above the trees.

* * * * * *

'So by means of the very welcome donations from the public, and funds raised by the many activities of this community, you actually manage to remain financially viable,' I asked the Right Reverend Leo Smith OSB PhD, Abbot of Buckfast Abbey.

'Just about,' he replied, with a twinkle in his eye.

'You get no endowments?'

He leaned back in his chair and smiled ruefully. 'Endowments... where from? I only wish we did!'

We were sitting in the private quarters of the old house adjacent to the Abbey. I knew this to be the only fully-restored medieval monastery in the whole of England and that it had flourished for over 500 years before being destroyed on orders from Henry VIII in 1539. I knew, too, that in 1882 a handful of Benedictine monks had returned to Buckfast and in 1907 set about reconstructing the Abbey Church on its original foundations: it had taken 31 years to complete, all the work being done by only four monks of whom one alone was a mason, helped occasionally by two others. I, like many many thousand visitors, had studied the photographs on the walls of the restaurant in the Abbey grounds, portraying that miracle. I had watched the beautifully produced video-programme telling of the work done and the way of life in the community, not only in the past, but here in the present day... so it was with something akin to awe that I looked again at Father Leo Smith.

'Out there', and I indicated the beautifully laid-out gardens, the Abbey Church across the way, the school, the restaurant and the complex of buildings which enclose the large private areas which the public do not see, including this old original house in which we were

55

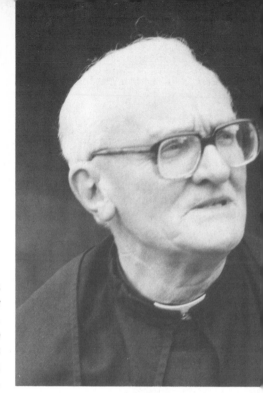

Far right: Buckfast Abbey. Built by four monks over a period of 31 years . . . and right, the present Abbot, the Right Reverend Leo Smith OSB PhD.

talking, '...all that must take an immense amount of hard work to be kept in this perfect state of maintenance. How many monks have you here at Buckfast?'

'At the moment we have a community of 41,' he replied, 'but of that 41 there are six more or less permanently out on parish and other work. For instance, two are on the parish at Cardiff, one being chaplain to the comprehensive school there. Another is chaplain to an old folks home at Brighton, and we have one as chaplain to a Benedictine Convent near Worcester, and two monks at Tavistock.'

'And do they,' I queried, 'undertake a set period of service outside, and then return here to the monastery?'

'It can be so. But once a man is fully integrated into a parish, well, there is little point in disturbing him unless, of course, something occurs which may change the situation.'

'And this monastery,' I asked, 'is also the parish Church?'

'Oh yes. One of the 27 priests here is appointed the parish priest. But to answer your original question, yes, it does take a big staff to keep it all running and above ground. A lot of hard work goes into

the maintenance and into keeping 40 odd monks reasonably clothed, fed and happy... but remember this is a working community and we raise a lot of funds from what we call our "industries". In summertime this consists of the visitors, and then there is the farm, our famous tonic wine and the bees.'

'Yes, about those bees,' I commented. 'I seem to recall there was a major theft some little while back in which the entire colony was removed?'

'Blown up out of all proportion by the media,' he laughed. 'We did have someone pilfering from the hives, but it was more of a nuisance than a major disaster. Brother Adam as you may know has worked for over 70 years on that side of our industry, and in truth it's hard enough without such irritations . . . you know we have 320 hives scattered within an area of ten miles from the Abbey, and another 500 up on the edge of the Moor at Sherberton. That is our queen-rearing centre and forms the nucleus of our whole beekeeping activities. We keep them up there because it is isolated and a hard environ which makes them tough and healthy survivors. Selected drones are isolated there . . . it is very unlikely that any marauding drone will reach them and interfere with the purity of the strain. But this last summer!' and he spread his hands in mock despair, 'has been a disaster. The cold spring wrought havoc.'

The geography of beekeeping set my mind questioning along a similar track. 'What was it,' I asked, 'that decided the original Cistercian monks in the eleventh century, to choose this site for a monastery. Was it the river?'

'Yes, but not only that. It was the shape of the place. You may be sure they were experienced architects and builders and this site was surveyed with great care. If you look at the monastery from the air you will see that it stands on a tongue of land formed by a loop in the river, and the high ground lies at the back. So the whole area all drains into the Dart, which overcomes at one blow the major problem of drainage. Then, of course, the river contained fish which undoubtedly formed a large part of the early monks' diet, and by the thirteenth century they were engaged in sheep farming for the wool.

'The first date we have for the foundation is 1018 but there may well have been something here prior to that, though there is no actual historical evidence of this. We found the Charter some years ago in Exeter, in which it is said that King Canute in 1018 granted the Sheriff of Devon the right to make a foundation here. Then the records seem to disappear, but it was re-founded about a century later in 1136 by some monks of Normandy who after another ten years were absorbed into the Cistercian Order. So Buckfast became Cistercian in 1146, and they surveyed the land and built in the usual pattern with the church to the north and the monastic buildings forming a quadrangle to the south.'

'How many monks would there have been here at that time?'

'Very difficult to say, but I do not think Buckfast was ever a very large monastery.'

'How long have you been Abbot, Father?'

'Nearly eleven years. This is my second term, since an Abbot is elected every eight years.'

'And the school. Are all the pupils Roman Catholics?'

'Most of them are, but we do not stipulate this. We just tell the parents that if they come here they will be treated like Catholics, except for the Sacraments and such like, of course, but they have to go to Church on Sundays and so forth. At the moment we have 110 pupils and most of them when they leave go to our Benedictine public schools. Downside, Douai, Belmont, and we also get them to Exeter, Taunton and Plymouth College.'

'Of the pupils who pass through the school, do a significant number become monks?'

'Not one, so far,' he laughed, 'since we opened the school in 1967.'

'And what would you say is the function of this community to-day?'

A smile flickered across his face. 'Well, that is difficult indeed to answer in a few words. A Benedictine community has always been a spiritual centre for the district, and we try to continue this. It is why we have done so much in recent years on the educational side—by which I'm not referring to the school here, but to the Heritage as we call it; trying to put out educational work for schools in general. We send out packs, and kits, and all that sort of thing, and the schools come, and the children walk around and eat buns... ask questions...' This most courteous gentleman looked straight at me, again with that twinkle in his eye.

'And that', I said, 'sends out vibrations into wider fields?'

'We hope so.'

I wandered back into the Abbey, held my camera against the glass protective wall behind the high altar, and took the photograph you see of the magnificent east window, the work of Dom Charles

East window in Buckfast Abbey Church, but go and see the richness of the colour.

Norris some twenty years ago. About 5,000 separate pieces of wonderfully coloured glass an inch thick, cemented each one to another. But ah! What a pale shadow this is of the real thing. You must go... you must go and feel the sheer force of that colour!

My mind wandered back to the river which, in a way, gave rise to the Abbey. In a fashion it could be seen as a reflection of a spiritual journey: it was born from the sky, and spends its lifetime flowing back to the ocean from whence it came. Then, who knows, it may possibly return to some different birthplace once more.

So I stood beneath the soaring stone arches and listened awhile to the silence in this hallowed place, marvelling at the sheer fulfilment of it all, and words which I had heard earlier in the day came echoing back: given the right people, in the right place, at the right time, almost anything may be achieved.

* * * * * *

When leaving the Abbey for Buckfastleigh you will see a sign on the left *Dart Valley Railway and Buckfast Butterfly Farm*. One does not normally associate farming with butterflies, but this fascinating project is attracting more and more visitors and becoming well-known throughout the country.

I was lucky in that Peter Wells, who at the time was deputising for the Managing Director David Field, was standing when I arrived at the turnstile of this 9,500 square feet of sub-tropical enclosed garden, casually watching a video-programme which was magnetising the visitors like a piece of sticky flypaper. Close alongside, the Dart followed tranquilly on her way but I did observe that yet another small leat had been bled off here, the water being conducted by pipes into an enormous glass greenhouse which forms the main building of the enterprise.

'What,' I asked Peter, 'is going on here? And most specifically, why the water supply from the river?'

'Come into the house', was his reply, 'and see the full story for yourselves.' My wife and I paid our entry fee of £1.80 each, passed through a swing door protected on the inside by a bird-deterring bead screen, and we started to sweat. Not surprising since the temperature was around 80 degrees Fahrenheit and tropically humid with it, but we forgot this immediately as a large Heliconius Charitonius impudently settled on a leaf not six inches from our noses and preened itself for inspection. Behind it, in full fruit-bearing splendour, two banana trees reared from a lush bed of exotic flowers and everywhere one looked some magnificently striped, spotted, camouflaged and obviously happy, healthy butterfly was busy about the sort of things butterflies busy themselves about. It was captivating.

'How many different species are there in here?' I queried, and Peter waxed almost lyrical.

'Probably up to 50 just at the moment... and there are about 500 of them flitting about in here getting on with the business of living. We have created a micro-environment of sub-tropic type, and this is not only for satisfaction of the visitors, it's an essential part of the whole breeding process because,' and he hesitated, looking at us closely, 'do you know anything about butterflies?'

'Nothing,' I said, 'except that they are beautiful to look at, fly, and do not bite.'

'Good,' he responded, 'and you're right on all three counts. We can start from the beginning then. The Centre, or "farm" as we call it, was opened in 1984 by a group of enterprising businessmen and is the only one of its kind in the South West. While it is, of course, at root a commercial venture and therefore has to show a profit at the end of the year, it is also of very great value as an educational and research project.

61

'Around November the butterflies leave here and the pupae all go to the Entomology department of Southampton University. They keep a small house there where the breeding is maintained and supply us with new pupae ready for the next season. They also, of course, supply us with a lot of technical "know how" should any particular problem arise, so there is a very happy relationship between we two organisations. It is not generally known, but the DNA molecule of the butterfly pupa is very similar to that of a human, so it is useful ground for genetic research.

'But to return to the farm here,' he continued. 'All the plants you see are very carefully chosen for two specific reasons. They must provide food for the final butterfly, but equally important—and this is not generally understood—the butterfly will only lay her eggs on a plant that the caterpillar can and will eat. They are not necessarily the same plant. We get lots of people asking why it is that, for instance, despite the fact that they have bountiful buddleia in the garden, the butterflies appear to be getting fewer. It is true, they *are* getting fewer, and one of the reasons is that, while the buddleia provides excellent nectar for sustaining the butterfly, it is useless to the caterpillar, so the butterfly will not lay her eggs there. If people would only reserve one small area of their garden—it need not be any larger than their dining table—and allow to grow there all the things we spend much time and effort removing from our gardens such as nettles, docks, wild grasses and the like, two things would result. First, they will have created a splendid little environment for the local butterflies to *breed* in, and secondly they will have a lovely addition to the garden in what amounts to a micro-culture of the local indigenous plants.

'David Field is very keen on this British Butterfly side of the business, and on educating the public on the requirements to maintain a healthy supply. We breed them, of course, here on the farm, but not for release into the wild.'

I was peering at a small notice near one of the tropical plants beside the path which read 'The Owl Butterfly likes to feed on rotting fruit which very often ferments, making them drunk!'

Left: Buckfast Butterfly Farm. Happy healthy butterflies busy about whatever butterflies busy themselves about . . . and by the hundreds!

'Quite like humans in things other than just genetic structure,' I commented, eyeing a magnificent—but rather stupid Monarch Danaus Plexippus gold and black specimen alighting on my wife's green and white floral print frock. 'How do you heat the place?'

'Gas. It's very expensive keeping this temperature and the humidity correct. We "flood" these gravel paths every morning, and of course, in answer to your original question, the water from the Dart out there supplies this large pool which also helps with the humidity.'

I studied the pool, which was covered with a cloth of healthy green pondweed. Out of it at odd places protruded the heads of exquisite little green terrapins, freshwater tortoises wearing contented dreamy expressions: life was obviously good. Meanwhile, around our feet, tiny Chinese quail strutted purposefully, and finches flew overhead.

'Why the birds?' I asked.

'Control of pests,' came the reply. 'It stands to reason that we cannot use any pesticides or insecticides so we have to do it in the natural manner. Believe me, it takes a lot of careful control because, due to the high temperature and humidity, pests do tend to proliferate. So we introduce selected birds which feed on the prevalent types, and the whole thing has to be kept in just the correct balance.'

I was beginning to realise that breeding and displaying about 50 different species of butterfly amounted to much more than growing a patch of stinging nettles.

'But we have achieved it,' Peter was saying. 'In the hothouse here the visitor can see the entire process: eggs, caterpillars, pupae, and the final butterfly. In fact you can, over here, watch the butterfly emerging from the pupa case.'

But I was looking, transfixed, at an unbelievably large specimen—some six inches across the wings—down in the corner of the case he was indicating, where about a hundred different pupae hung in palpitating expectancy. It was coloured like a Persian carpet with furry symmetrical designs ending at the wingtips in what looked like opposed snakes' heads, complete with eyes.

'Ah, *that*', said Peter, 'is the Attacus Atlas, a Giant Atlas moth. We keep him in there.'

I didn't ask why.

'I'll bet the children love it,' I commented.

64

'A Paradise for them,' came the reply. 'We run a full education programme here for schools, catering right through the age-groups from pre-school upwards, and we also cater for handicapped children. The educational side runs right through primary, secondary, and even up to "A" level genetics. There is a classroom available here and, though I say it myself, we do provide a splendid educational "package" which is sent to schools making enquiries. A teacher may select any appropriate facet of the whole and the children then come here and are given an introductory lecture by a member of the staff. They may see a video programme, and then go on to study whatever area is appropriate for them. We have groups attending as small as five or six, and up to fifty or sixty.'

'What sort of numbers of the public do you get attending in a normal season?' I asked.

'This year it will be around 150,000: there is undoubtedly a growing interest in this field.'

But I was absorbed in watching an ant carrying a piece of detached leaf laboriously toward its underground home, all perfectly demonstrated in another glass case with detailed explanation of what it was doing and why on little notices stuck in the soil. It was all so well organised that I enquired whether the ants themselves had written the notices. Peter showed me to the door.

Well worth visiting, this butterfly farm, and outside, within a stone's throw of the farm, is another activity linked to this incredible river—the Dart Valley Steam Railway— where, shunting and hissing and the nostalgic smell of coalburning bring home to us that we are, perhaps, getting on a little in years... for these are things of another, more elegant and predictable age. Steam trains: ah, childhood joys!

* * * * * *

The Dart Valley Light Railway PLC is responsible for perpetuating a piece of English heritage. Steam trains—the very sound, smell and feel of them and the coaches they hauled—are dear to a great many hearts, and on the two lines now run by this company you may literally take a journey into the past. What is more, much of it is

Dart Valley Light Railway PLC is responsible for perpetuating a piece of English Heritage. Michael Henderson the Publicity Manager.

done alongside whole stretches of the Dart from which quite magnificent views may be obtained. One line starts at Buckfastleigh and runs via Staverton to Totnes. The other runs from Paignton in Torbay via Churston to Kingswear from where you may take the ferry to Dartmouth. Michael Henderson, the publicity manager, talked to me about the company while I examined the railway museum with him at Buckfastleigh.

'At any time during the season we will have two steam locomotives in use here on the Buckfast line, and three on the Torbay line. This is really the minimum we have to have fully operational in the season to ensure an effective service. But of course we have many more steam engines, eighteen in all, and in addition four diesel engines. These are either undergoing maintenance here in our heavy repair workshops at Buckfast, or in the light maintenance workshop at Paignton. Some of these, of course, are on "stand-by".

'What we try to reproduce', Michael continued, 'from the moment you walk on to the station and buy your ticket, is as near an atmosphere of the Great Western Railway as it was in the great days of steam. In this we have been so successful that films and television serials, among them *Hound of the Baskervilles*, *A Horseman Riding By* and *Penmarric* have been shot at Staverton station just down the line from here. This line opened in 1969, while the Torbay to Kingswear line opened in 1973. Of course the whole business has to pay its way, and when you bear in mind that we employ some 26 full-time staff which more or less doubles at the height of the season when we take on additional staff for a multitude of duties, plus the rolling stock maintenance, you will appreciate that our overheads are quite high. But we are splendidly supported in much of the work by two voluntary organisations, the Dart Valley Railway Association and the Torbay and Dartmouth Railway Society, whose members put in an enormous amount of time for the sheer love of it.

'The tracks were originally part of the British Rail network, of course, and we were able to use much of the remaining equipment. But a lot of work was involved in bringing the lines back into serviceable order. The gauge is standard for the Great Western—4 feet 8½ inches between the lines.

'The coaches are, in fact, a bigger problem than the actual locomotives, because all passenger coaches prior to the 1950s were insulated with asbestos between the carriage "skins"... and you know the situation with regard to that material today. It is perfectly safe so long as it remains undisturbed there between the "skins" but difficulties arise if we need to strip a coach down for repair work: and remember all rolling stock has to be maintained to the full standard of British Rail.

'We have seven standard coaches here at Buckfast, and about double that number on the Torbay line. In addition we have three genuine Victorian coaches fitted out as faithfully as possible in the original style. Since an average coach takes some sixty passengers, an engine hauling, say, five coaches is carrying some 300 people. This year, 1986, we have carried some 75,000 passengers on the Buckfast line, and about double that on the Torbay line. In fact we have recently instituted a combined rail and river trip on one ticket. When you buy the ticket you also get a trip up the river, maybe from Dartmouth to Totnes, depending on the tide.'

I can vouch for the fact that a trip on the steam train is a splendid way to see the river, for the track hugs it closely from Buckfast to Totnes, while the Torbay line completes the last one and a half miles actually on the river bank before terminating at Kingswear.

'Yes, the whole enterprise has been a huge success,' Michael continued, bubbling with an enthusiasm which was catching. 'Last season we fairly burst at the seams trying to pack the passengers in, and now we are extending our activities because we realise that when a family comes out for a day of steaming nostalgia they need something to do having got off the train. So in addition to the railway museum here, and the maintenance workshops where you may watch the locomotives actually being serviced, not to mention the old original style signal box which has gone forever on the main lines, we are developing an entire leisure centre with gardens, a lovely riverside walk and picnic grounds with children's play area plus a mini golf course and a maze. It all makes for a really worthwhile day.'

So I left him, standing against a notice which read: 'RIGHTS OF WAY ACT, 1932. THE GREAT WESTERN RAILWAY COMPANY HEREBY GIVE NOTICE THAT THIS WAY IS NOT DEDICATED TO THE PUBLIC'. You can turn history upside-down, I thought, in the fullness of time!

We must follow the river yet farther toward its mouth, aware as we do so that for much of the voyage we may be accompanied by the near-forgotten sound of a distant steam whistle, and that wonderful accelerating beat of escaping steam as a *real* locomotive gathers speed, and maybe just occasionally that irreplaceable smell of coal smoke and hot oil all of which, but for this enterprising company, might well have disappeared forever some two decades ago.

* * * * * *

On this next stretch we begin to get the feel of a lowland river. The Dart has emerged from the border country belt which I have described as a 'penumbra of transition' and it is hereabouts that the transition manifests itself powerfully in man's activities. The river's first youth is spent. It has gathered experience and from here on seems, as it were, to generate creative occupations based on that maturity and influence. We are entering the cider country, and an area that has long supported industry based on water-mill power, and art in all its forms flowers here, for just downstream is Dartington Hall—surely a powerhouse of creative thinking.

From Buckfastleigh the river flows south in close company with road and railway, to pass under both Dart and Austin's bridges. The latter we know dates back to the 1300s. In fact Austin's bridge is well worth looking at, with five splendid arches, but alas the close proximity of Buckfastleigh sewage works does somewhat detract from an otherwise beautiful environ. The A384 shortly leaves the river to serve Weston and Stretchford, while the railway having passed beneath the road remains faithfully hugging the east bank as both sweep round Derry's Copse.

Eastward lies the parish of Staverton, which name comes from the original 'Staen-a-ford Tun' meaning 'settlement on a stony ford', and it was while walking up from the railway line at Knapper's Crossing—named after a much respected lady crossing-keeper of old—that I spied looking down at me from the bottom of St Paul de Leon's churchyard a commanding wooden statue. I hurried into the church and there found a fascinating little booklet which you may buy for a few pence, written by the Reverend C.A. Cardale, Vicar of Staverton, who kindly gave me permission to quote therefrom. It deals with the statue, which is of the Madonna and Child, and I find the story intriguing.

Apparently a Mr Douglas Rouse, on finding a log drifted up on a small island in the river hereabouts, back in 1970 set about carving the statue to help pass the hours. When completed he mounted the carving in a commanding position on the island, surrounding it with stones from the riverbed. He then left the area, being of a somewhat nomadic inclination. You may not be surprised that the lifesize figure became a matter of 'some local interest, and gradually its fame spread more widely. The local Press ran a feature on it and strangers from abroad began to make visits to this mysterious statue which has considerable power. Then, unaccountably, the Madonna disappeared. Nobody I have been able to contact knows exactly how or why but it seems likely that rising flood waters might have dislodged it and carried it downstream.

Certainly some months later a gentleman found the statue in the river below Totnes and, with an amount of energy matching his artistic appreciation, hauled it off to decorate his house. But the parishioners of Staverton had by now gained a proprietorial affection for 'their' statue and wished to have it returned to the

Far right: Madonna and
Child, carved from a drifting
log by Douglas Rouse, and
right, his powerful work
'Christ with Arms Uplifted'.

parish. Negotiations took place and a sum was raised as recompense
for the cost and time taken in the recovery, whereupon the statue
was duly returned to Staverton and placed in the tower of St Paul de
Leon Church until a suitable site be agreed. Eventually it was
decided to place it overlooking the road beneath, so this lovely
statue which, though somewhat crude in form, does nevertheless
possess a remarkable fluency of line and expression, may now be
seen by anyone passing.

Mr Rouse was later found and consulted, and stated that he was
quite happy with the situation and enjoyed making such
carvings—it gave the public, he said, something to look at. I take
this opportunity to compliment you, Mr Rouse, wherever you may
be, for your handiwork is an asset. Following up the story with my
Sherlock Holmes hat firmly in place I got scent of another of your
carvings in which if I'm not mistaken, I detect an element of—
rebellion? It stands on a prominent bluff at the disused Penn Recca
slate mine and portrays 'Christ, with Arms Uplifted'. More than
lifesize it must have been a commanding work in its original form

Dartington Hall.

but alas, it rotted through at the base and lay for some time supine until a band of outraged parishioners reinstated it upright, albeit buried up to the knees. Strangely, it seems thus to be making a yet more powerful statement. I read your message, Mr Rouse, and hope that I have spelt your name correctly, for there is a difference of opinion about it locally. You may see the statue, on the quarry edge overlooking Lower Combe in Landscove, but put on a watertight pair of boots if you wish to pay homage.

Halfway between Buckfastleigh and Totnes the A384 takes a fiendish twist to cross both river and railway at Riverford Bridge. Railway and river then again leave the road to pass under Staverton Bridge and loop round the Dartington estate.

Dartington Hall has been occupied for some 1,000 years and more and over much of that period has exerted its influence far and wide. Today, under the direction of the Dartington Hall Trust, that influence in the field of industry and art is every bit as far-reaching, for it offers a wide range of courses to over 400 students each year, while the 1,000 or so acres of land within the estate form the basis of two farm-sharing projects. The Trust's business interests include boatbuilding, cider, glass and furniture making, and the Dartington College of Arts which is run in conjunction with the Devon County Council provides courses in Art and Design, Music and Theatre. Its educational facilities include the Dartington Tech which operates in the field of Youth Training and Adult Education.

The size and scope of its current operations may be judged by the fact that the Trust employs some 500 people in a unique organisation which has grown steadily since Leonard and Dorothy Elmhirst bought the badly run-down estate and medieval Hall in 1925. Dorothy Elmhirst was one of the Whitney-Straight family, which was much involved in the laying down of the railway network in the USA. It was chiefly her money which financed the Dartington venture, and their joint drive and vision which has resulted in the present magnificent home for what can only be described as a powerhouse of culture.

Earliest mention of the original house is in a Royal Charter of 833 AD, and this was assigned after the Conquest to a colleague of William the Conqueror, one William de Falaise. The church tower which stands in the grounds is thought to date from the twelfth

The Twelve Apostles in Dartington Grounds.

century, built by the Fitz Martins who were wealthy Westcountry landowners. In 1348 the house reverted to the Crown and 36 years later Richard II presented it to his half-brother, John Holland. It was he who made Dartington into a large country house with layout much as we see it today. The quadrangle was at that time completely enclosed, and the buildings housed some 60 odd knights and squires who made up the Holland household. The Hollands lost the estate during the Wars of the Roses after which it was forfeited to the Crown and held by a number of tenants until purchased by Sir Arthur Champernowne whose successors kept it for nearly 400 years. Much of the private house was modernised during the eighteenth century but the agricultural depression of the nineteenth century eroded away the fortunes of that family and, as I have said, when the Elmhirsts bought the estate in 1925 the buildings were little short of a ruin.

The great Banqueting Hall, which perhaps makes the most impact on any visitor, had been roofless for more than 100 years. Ivy climbed up and out of the empty windows and the floor was covered in coarse grass. The task of refurbishing the place must have been daunting indeed, but it was planned in detail and efficiently executed. In 1931 timber was cut from the estate and fashioned into exact replicas of the original roof beams and the present roof overlaid. The Hall measures 80 by 40 feet and the fireplace at one end is seventeen feet in width. This alone gives one some idea of the style in which the original owners lived, and anyone who has had the privilege of attending a course at Dartington which involves living on the estate for a short while will know to what it is I refer when speaking of the atmosphere of the place.

To sit in the gardens behind the Hall in the cool of a summer evening with sunlight gilding those elegant facades of stone, while all about one are exquisitely kept lawns, shadowed by the regal trees and shrubs, is a balm to the soul. Will you let it, history then takes you gently by the hand and makes you aware of the debt we owe to the Elmhirsts and their like: people who have the vision and are prepared to finance the regeneration of such places so that, hopefully, they may once more stand on their own feet financially, to remain a lasting example of what, beneath all the cheap and merely functional, the expedient and shoddy froth that drifts across our land today, is the real and lasting England.

There is a lovely view of the river down in the valley if you take

The Totnes to Buckfastleigh train. The Dart Valley railway hugs the river bank.

the road through the estate which joins the A384 just north of Totnes. Indeed, there is the ancient port ahead, and it is from the weir just north of the town that the river becomes tidal, so perhaps from here on our exploration had best be done from my canoe, for there is no better manner of seeing a waterway.

75

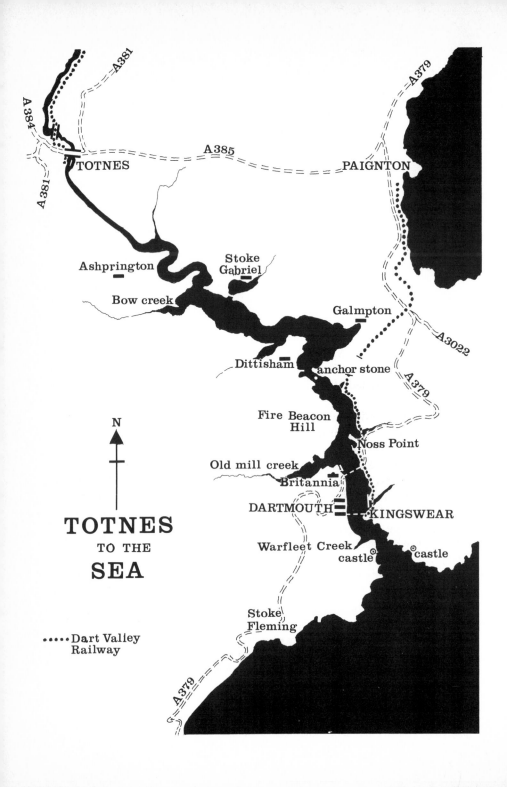

IV
Totnes to the Sea

I cannot tell what ye say, rosy rocks,
I cannot tell what ye say;
But I know that there is a spirit in you
And a word in you this day.

Charles Kingsley

Geoffrey of Monmouth, writing his *Historia Britonium* in the twelfth century, tells how one Brutus, son of Sylvius, grandson of Aeneas the Trojan, killed his father while out hunting and was expelled from Italy. After settling in Greece this worthy conquered the Trojans and led them in an army to defeat the Grecian King Pendrasu.

You may wonder what all this has to do with Totnes? Have patience; the results of distant and seemingly irrelevant facts can have a dreadful way of coming to roost in one's own backyard. Pendrasu's daughter wed our Brutus—what a companionable lot they were—and her father, by way of a dowry I imagine, presented Brutus with a whacking great fleet of ships, fully provisioned and ready for sea. Could it have been a hint? Anyway the Trojans, with Brutus at the prow, sailed away to seek their fortunes... as good a way as any of getting rid of one's troublesome son-in-law with a deal of flair and panache.

After a few adventures in what we now call France this aggressive character, clearly one of the 'dominant five per cent', finding the prevailing winds favourable to yet further exploits, sailed on until his fleet was brought up all-standing on the coast of southwest England. In those times, if we are to believe the historians, this whole area was referred to as 'Totnes' and was thought to be inhabited by 'a few giants'. Brutus promptly named the place Britain in order to perpetuate his own ego. I can believe it, for surely

anyone with the energy, drive and ambition of this man could never be judged humble.

I have often pondered how much the fact that we sailors—most particularly the early sailors—preferred running with the wind than beating against it . . . how much that fact has fashioned the fortunes of nations. Arrived at our coastline this redoubtable man found it much to his liking and 'forced the giants to fly into the caves of the mountains' to quote Geoffrey. Under his direction the Trojans then set about dividing up the land between themselves.

It is plain that, while fossicking along this coast, his ships found the deepwater estuary of Dartmouth. What is more natural than that they should blow yet further with those winds, and drift with the flood tide up this attractive river for some ten miles or so to the area we now know as Totnes town, by which time their keels had probably run hard and fast on the mud. At any rate this conquering hero is said here to have disembarked with those famous words which have reverberated down the centuries: 'Here I stand, and here I rest, and this good town shall be called Totnes.'

Well, that sums up a 1,000 and more years of history very smartly, disposes of any doubts as to why we are British, and explains the origins of Totnes. You may enquire just how this canoeist, with tongue-in-cheek, knows all these wonderful 'historical' facts? Indeed, how does he know anything of Totnes on the Dart, since he comes from that heathen place across the border: Cornwall? It is because he, too, is a sailor and as such drove the keel of his own vessel hard and fast on the mud, taking care to do it at high water springs just above the bridge.

Then, in a way sailors seem to be able, he bearded the Totnes Archivists in their den—quite a lot of them—and made pertinent enquiries. He ate cakes in excellent tea-houses, walked the streets and browsed in the 'Narrows' and elsewhere while tracing the ancient walls of the original medieval town surrounding the castle. He made friends with the late proprietors of the sadly disappeared Seymour Hotel at the Bridge and gawped at the utterly banal monument to William John Wills who was born at number 3 on the Plains—why is it we always seem to end up with blunt phallic obelisks when we wish to honour someone? Typically Brutish—and

Left: East Gate, Totnes.

**Jo and Barry Weekes. 'We put our joint talents to
work and produced "Spirit of Totnes" which presents
the rich heritage of the town to visitors.'**

then, on the advice of the Chief Archivist who was understandably
becoming fed-up with this twentieth-century invader, bought that
most excellent little book by the late Percy Russell FSA, and
published by the Devonshire Association of 7, The Close, Exeter,
and sat down and read it from cover to cover.

It is fascinating. You will learn more of Totnes from those pages
than I have either the room or the inclination to tell you. Buy the
paperback, second impression, then walk down High Street and
pass under the lovely arch which was the original town's east gate
into Fore Street. Stand there on the Brutus Stone sunk into the
pavement . . . and I tell you your heart will warm to the people of
this town, as mind did. You might even, if you are lucky, happen
upon the Information Booth where you may pick up, as I did, a
small leaflet entitled *The Spirit of Totnes: a visual and sound
experience illustrating the rich and varied heritage of the town.* Just

what I need, thought I, and with journalistic nose twitching set off hot-foot to the Mansion House where the programme was even then showing to the general public—and free at that!

Alas, the show had already half-run but I asked the lady at the door whether, perchance, there would be any objection to my tape-recording the sound-track since likely as not there would be some interesting snippets to include in my book. She looked a little nonplussed, swallowed once or twice, rose from her chair and, drawing herself visibly upward said with unmistakable emotion words to the effect of: 'No, you certainly may NOT. I think you've got a thundering cheek. Do you imagine my husband and I have spent untold hours creating this programme so that the likes of you can come and plagiarise it? Go and do your own research!' And then she visibly deflated and added: '...Oh, I *do* so hate having to tell people off!'

My heart warmed to her. There are limits to how much you may transgress every code of ethics in the book and I admitted it and apologised, then waited until the next programme was due to start and—without my tape-recorder— entered the hall. For the next twenty minutes, by virtue of sheer technological brilliance, artistic flair, and three simultaneously-operating slide projectors plus a wizardry of original music and commentary I was transported through history, taken back in time visually and in sound to absorb the heritage of the place, accompanied throughout by a ghostly cloaked figure who, without uttering one word, directed my attention to salient points. But I recognised her face!

Jo and Barry Weekes, of the Photographic Studio, 31 Bridgetown, came to Totnes from Dulverton in 1980. Each of them in their different ways was involved with the Arts. Jo came to the College here as a student of Theatre, while Barry travelled to Plymouth College of Art to study photography.

'Jo did four years at the college,' Barry told me as we sat over tea and buns in their rooms above the studio, 'while I completed two years at Plymouth and then, with our degrees "in the bag" so to speak, we set about searching for centres where we might employ the skills we had acquired. In the process we visited Telford's famous iron bridge, a living memorial up there in the Black Country to the great industrial revolution. It was quite obvious to us that industrial archaeology had been made into a major tourist attraction. The heritage of that area was being presented, and presented well, to the modern visitors. So we asked each other: "Isn't this an area in which we can put our own talents to work?'"

'And Totnes seemed the place to do it?' I prompted.

'Well,' said Jo, handing me another current bun, 'this place just cast a spell over us and we decided to stay. We committed ourselves to the commercial venture you have seen below—that brings in the bread and butter—and meanwhile began to work on the programme you saw portraying the ancient Borough. The town has been dependent on the river for a 1,000 years and more, and it is all still going on around us. As we gained more and more knowledge of the area and its history it became clear that there was an opening for us to present it all to the visitors who come each summer.'

'Of course there were the guide books,' added Barry, 'and other sources which we studied thoroughly. All the information was there but nowhere was it presented in an audio/visual form. So we set ourselves a brief: to inform the visitor who was already in the town and looking for information. You see,' he went on reflectively, 'Totnes has no problem attracting folk . . . they come in flocks. The problem, it seemed to us, was handling them when they arrived. So that, in a nutshell, is what we did. The South Hams District Council, having seen the programme gave us a grant and the show is put on in the Mansion House daily. We hope that in the years to come it will continue showing for we do believe that it helps the visitor to absorb the unique atmosphere of the place.'

I agreed. I hope you, reader, will also one day be led by that atmospheric figure in the long cloak and hood—a transformed Jo Weekes—through the centuries. I hope, too, that you will appreciate the sheer brilliance of the photography, the masterly handling of the three computer-controlled simultaneous slide-projectors backed by stero music and commentary. As they dissolve the images they seem to dissolve time itself. The programme is a work of art, and not to be missed.

So I walked back across the bridge, built in 1828 to replace its medieval predecessor, by Charles Fowler who, incidentally, is responsible for the original Covent Garden in London. As I paddled down past Vere Island I looked at the town with new eyes and, let's be honest, no little affection. I like Totnes.

Right: Low tide at Vere Island, Totnes. Every stone, every building, can tell a story.

The Anchor Stone off Dittisham. Sir Walter Raleigh
is reputed to have frequently smoked a quiet
pipe thereon.

I fairly shot down with an increasing ebb tide and got stuck on the
mud in Bow Creek which was unfortunate—and I hope Michael
Williams, publisher of Bossiney Books, did not feel his ears burning
back there in Cornwall, for there is nothing like an ocean of mud
twixt you and the shore to encourage eloquence. On the next tide I
canoed up to Stoke Gabriel on the north bank and all but came to
grief on the sill which dams the mouth of the creek.

Stoke Gabriel has been the home since time immemorial of salmon
fishing on this river. In fact it may well have been the convenience
for fishing that resulted in the village growing on the north bank of
this small tidal creek. The fish are netted as they swim up-river
between mid-March and mid-August, and there are stringent
restrictions operating, as everywhere else on the Dart, to prevent
over fishing. Anyone wishing to fish these waters, whether it be for
salmon, trout or freshwater fish (including eels) should first obtain a
current South West Water Licence and permission to fish from the
owners of the fishing. Prospective fishermen are strongly advised to

obtain a current copy of the S.W. Water's *Guide to Angling and Recreation* available from Peninsula House, Rydon Lane, Exeter EX2 7HR. This gives details of cost for season, week or day fishing along the Dart and to whom application should be made for the different areas. Woe to the poacher, whether it be by rod and line, net, or the more recent spear-gun!

The river takes a northerly slant now past a lovely example of Regency architecture at Sandridge, then sweeps south in front of Waddeton, another fine mansion built in 1820 and, ah! . . . already I can smell the sea. The banks are drawing farther apart ahead as though the river were spreading its arms in welcome. In summertime hereabouts it is wonderfully flanked by green woods which tumble down to lean far out over the water . . . and there is a spicy new quality in that water for it is very brackish now and tells a wondrous tale. On stony banks under those green canopies of leaves, up each and every small tributary and fold of its shores,comes a whispering of unimaginable stretches of ocean. The river feels the salty strangeness of it and merges with awe and a sense of a long-forgotten feeling for that place from which it originally came. There is joy in the recollection, and a glad acceptance. So the current quickens, and the river widens yet more, flowing steadily on down to what by any assessment must be judged one of the most beautiful, romantic and historic harbours on our English coastline.

But what is this? After rounding Lower Gurrow Point, as I pass Viper's Quay at Dittisham where the river narrows after sweeping across the Flat Owers off Galmpton Creek, in the centre of the fairway is a sort of aquatic traffic island with splendid red topmark. It is the Anchor Stone, a weed-covered rock on which if we are to believe our forbears Sir Walter Raleigh was wont to sit and smoke a quiet pipe. If he did he would certainly have had to keep a wary eye lifting for the tide, since in those days there was no topmark and the Stone is completely immersed at high water. But you may be sure that exalted gentleman was alert to such a predictable ducking. Certainly more so than the later captain of the *William*, which boat struck the Stone when the latter was just beneath the surface, and sank. But that was some time back; probably about the period when, according to the old folk of Dittisham, they used to maroon on the rock any troublesome wives until the sight of the rising water made them more companionable. A practical answer to what is, after all, a problem still not unknown? From this arose the nickname 'Scold Stone' by which you may occasionally hear it called.

We are indeed paddling through hallowed waters. On the west bank, from Dittisham down to Mill Creek and beyond is the estate belonging today to the great—and great to the power of thirteen—grandchild of Sir Walter Raleigh himself, on the female side. I traversed the track behind Firebeacon Hill down past Bozomzeal Farm to pass a pleasant half-hour with that lady over a jug of tea. Sarah and Duncan Green live at Hole Farm which looks straight down a deep valley into Old Mill Creek. It was late afternoon as we talked and lights were beginning to wink on pontoons below the Naval College.

'The estate,' Sarah told me, 'was purchased from the Seale family at Dartmouth in 1873. Originally the Raleigh family had their residence at Mount Boone House where the College now stands. But the Royal Navy had for many years been searching for a more suitable and permanent place to house their young officers under training than the two hulks which were anchored off Mill Creek down there. The blighters issued a purchase order for the house and the land on which it stood. Despite vigorous objection by the Raleigh family the Admiralty threatened to seize the land under a compulsory purchase order... the first, incidentally, ever to be issued in England. The family took legal advice and sued the government without success. So the College was built, and Edward Raleigh and his family left Dartmouth in a towering rage and never returned. Soon after this Edward died and his son, Walter, also died intestate leaving a widow and one child called Mary Dorothea who, after considerable litigation inherited the Devonshire estate from her father. Mary Dorothea was my mother.

'It all then becomes a bit complicated,' the vivacious dark-haired Sarah explained with a twinkle, while two collies, a labrador and a black cat with collar individually and together sized up this stranger sitting at their table, and a telephone shrilled continually in the background. 'You see, the terms of Edward Ward Walter Raleigh's will made in 1867 entailed the estate to the legally begotten male issue of his nephew, Edward Walter Raleigh, forever... but added that should his nephew die without legally begotten male issue, the property should then pass to his sister's eldest son, Walter Raleigh Amesbury. The Amesbury family contested the inheritance, but the judge found rather in favour of

Mary Dorothea Raleigh. On her marriage to her first husband in 1922 the estate was placed into Trust for each of her children in equal parts, and this is the case today, though much of the estate business is run by a family limited company. With the death of Walter Frederick Carew Raleigh in 1906 the line became extinct. But the name of Raleigh, and the blood of the Raleighs, continues through the female line.'

'Yes,' I thought, looking at her, 'and here I can see something of the fire and drive that made that illustrious ancestor what he was. Genes are remarkable things... long may they last!'

'Have you sailed up Old Mill Creek yet?' Sarah was asking.

'Not yet,' I told her. 'That's on the books for tomorrow if the weather holds. I propose paddling from Dittisham to the river mouth.'

'Paddling?'

'I'm doing this navigable part in my canoe, it's by far the best way. I've just canoed right round the coastline of Cornwall, so this inland protected water makes a pleasant change.'

'Have another cup of tea.'

'Well,' she continued, putting six more teabags in the pot, 'there's a bit of history up there—or so we believe.'

'Tell me all.'

'The *Madre de Dios*, a Portuguese carrick, that's a merchant sailing ship, was captured by Sir Walter's "mob" and a skeleton crew put aboard. She was brought into Dartmouth as a prize, but meanwhile Sir Walter had been clapped into the Tower of London... you may know the story?'

'Roughly,' I said. 'Things haven't changed much.'

'Well, the crew were not happy and started distributing her cargo piecemeal to all their friends in this locality. Spices. Equipment and... who knows, the odd doubloon or whatever.'

'Escudos?' I queried.

'By all means,' she smiled, 'anyway Robert Cecil was sent with a posse of soldiers to control them but the crew—they were a pretty rough lot you understand—told them to take up knitting or something of the sort. In the end Raleigh had to be released and brought personally to reinstate some sort of discipline. This he did, and the *Madre de Dios* was then—and I quote— "taken up a nearby Creek" and scuttled. The obvious Creek,' Sarah mused, 'is Mill Creek down there. In fact it is almost certain to have been that

Creek for it is the only one deep enough. At any rate an aerial photograph taken recently has disclosed a "shadow" in the mud which looks remarkably like the lines of a sizeable ship.'

'So?' I queried.

'We're going to become mudlarks,' she laughed.

I wished her all success. Unlikely, of course, that a prize ship would be scuttled and left to rot with anything of value still aboard; nevertheless it is all very interesting and might yet prove to be one more link with historic events which will reverberate as long as there's an England.

* * * * * *

You may be sure I did paddle up Old Mill Creek when the tide served, and found a most romantic hulk rotting on the north bank, but this is the *Invermore* an old three-masted trading ship from Arklow which, when some 25 years back had finished her commercial service, was bought by an adventurous group who proposed sailing to Australia in her. Things went sadly wrong, and there she has lain ever since. Farther up the creek, though I peered hopefully into the shallow waters, I found no 'shadows' save that of my own slim craft down there on the bottom.

Dartmouth ahead: from Higher Noss Point on the east bank you may already see a forest of masts in the marina at Kingswear and the buildings of the town opposite. The trees which cover the southern shore of Old Mill Creek slope sharply up from the waterline, and ah... I find myself wondering whether occasionally in the wind there is heard the ghostly echo of a bo's'n's pipe and perhaps the faint beat of a long-gone Quarterdeck Marine Band? I am floating in the exact spot where the wooden hull of the original *HMS Britannia*, ship of the line, was finally moored in 1863. With masts removed she had, elsewhere, served as a training ship for young naval officer cadets. Her first berth in Portsmouth had been found unsuitable on account of far too many temptations ashore, and a second base at Portland had also proved unworkable due to its exposed position.

Dartmouth was ideal, for it not only offered a sheltered berth close to shore for the old high-sided hulk, but also plenty of land adjacent which was suitable for recreation. The land proved very suitable indeed for more than just recreation, as we have seen, but

Remains of "Invermore", desolate on the mud of Old
Mill Creek.

for all the high-handed methods used I cannot help feeling that it is
entirely appropriate that the present shore-based *Britannia* Royal
Naval College should stand where the original house of the Raleigh
family looked down on this lovely harbour.

In 1864 the two-decker *Hindostan* was positioned just ahead of
Britannia to provide more accommodation, a covered gangway
linking the two ships. It was by no means a chance decision
prompted by the attraction of the land adjacent to the two training
ships that persuaded the Admiralty to finally put down permanent
roots in Dartmouth. The port was of great strategic importance in
the days of the first Queen Elizabeth. Nine Dartmouth ships had
sailed to help scatter the Armada, and one of the first Spanish
prizes was brought here in triumph. The harbour only ceased to be a
leading naval base when the first class ships of the line became too
large for its anchorages. In 1869 the original *Britannia* was replaced
by a brand new part-completed ship which had never seen service,

**Britannia Royal Naval College. Passing-Out Parade
31 July 1986.**

having been made obsolete even as she was being built by the first
of the new breed of 'ironclads'.

At that time the full course of training by the cadets was
completed in two years, but all was far from well aboard those two
hulks. Despite attempts at improved conditions outbreaks of
smallpox and scarlet fever made it quite clear that such restricted
conditions for so many young recruits was not ideal. More space
was needed with sanitary conditions, and the powers responsible
already had their eyes on those sloping fields with the house atop, to
the south of Old Mill Creek.

By 1875 it had to be acknowledged that somewhere, and fairly soon, a training college would have to be built ashore. There was a lot of discussion in committee, and twenty more years passed while things got steadily worse aboard the hulks. In 1895 three cadets died during a serious outbreak of measles and pneumonia, which is not really surprising for conditions aboard must have been close to Hell. One may imagine, after the cramped and probably foetid quarters of the trainees, the effect of sudden exposure in boats to the blistering winds which sear down the river in winter. Hygiene in those days left much to be desired and it was quite clear to the authorities that things were just not good enough for the Senior Service.

The decision to move ashore was finally taken in March 1896, but it was another two years before the title deeds to the land finally changed hands. In 1900 a tender of just under £221,000 was accepted for the main building of the present college and Aston Webb, one of the foremost architects of that time, was commissioned to draw up the plans. In September 1905 the college opened and within two years was fully operational with a term of around 340 cadets. The staff was a mixture of naval and civilian instructors, 30 in all under the Headmaster Cyril Ashford who had been transferred from the naval training college at Osborne in the Isle of Wight. By 1914 the requirement for training ever increasing numbers of cadets demanded a virtual doubling of the college's accommodation and a whole new construction to house more classrooms, better laboratories and a proper masters' common room was added.

Recently Dartmouth College has broadened the scope of its intake to embrace Royal Marines, Chaplains, Instructor Officers, WRNS Officers, Medical and Dental Officers and Russian Interpreters, among others. Today cadets under instruction here are taught by some 63 naval officers and 31 lecturers.

So there the college stands, and nobody visiting the Dart or Dartmouth can for long remain unaware of its presence, for it presides on the hilltop like a spread of raspberry mousse flecked with clotted cream, a splendid monument to late Victorian architecture in an incomparable position looking down over green lawns falling to the harbour town and river. By appointment I was granted an interview with the First Officer WRNS who deals with public relations, and one September afternoon walked through the gates and up that imposing slope to cross the historic parade ground. The security was mind-boggling but once my credentials were cleared every facility was proffered and a free hand allowed me to photograph whatever and wherever I chose.

'In 1980, when Prince Andrew passed out of the college, the Queen took the salute there on the parade ground,' the publicity officer told me. 'You see,' she continued, 'at the end of the Spring Term each year the passing out parade known as the Lord High Admiral's Divisions is held. The Queen took the title of Lord High Admiral in 1964 and consequently at that Divisions it is either she or her personal representative who takes the salute. In 1981 we had the Queen Mother, then Princess Alexandra followed by Princess Anne. In April this year, 1986, we had the Duchess of Kent: you realise that between 150 and 250 officers pass out to the fleet at these parades? In fact the college has to curtail its number of trainees just now, for we have on the roll today almost 600 people.'

Splendid, I thought. We have seen what appears to be an alarming decline lately in the number of fighting ships available to defend our island, but it is good to know that the training continues—and of a standard second-to-none.

So I went and inspected the pristine white figurehead of the first floating *Britannia* and looked up at the White Ensign flying there far above the parade ground: and 44 years vanished like magic. Suddenly, I was back in another land-based naval training ship, *HMS Collingwood* as a very Ordinary and very very apprehensive Seaman looking a full-blown war in the face, and found myself reminiscing on the momentous events that had followed from my own decision, so long ago, to join the Royal Navy.

* * * * * *

Below the college the trees on the west bank thin out, and once past the naval pontoons with their lines of neatly parked dinghies, one comes to the Dart Marina backed by the modern Marina Hotel. It is from here that the car ferry known as 'higher ferry' connects the A379 across to a slipway on the Kingswear side of the river. Officers and cadets from the college would, in olden days, have crossed to embark near this slipway on the Great Western railway line for destinations en-route to London. The small and rather unprepossessing shelter of 'Britannia Halt' still stands beside the line and doubtless could it speak it might tell many a tale.

The Duchess of Kent inspecting one of the Passing-Out
Platoons at the Royal Naval College in April 1986.

This single-track line now runs, as I have said, from Paignton
only. Having emerged from Greenway Tunnel and passed over the
elegant stone Maypool viaduct just east of the Anchor Stone up-
river, it hugs the bank all the way to its terminus at Kingswear; of
which fact Kingswear is justly proud, for Dartmouth opposite is not
so served.

You may come to Dartmouth by rail, using the ferry to cross the
river, or by car direct, or on foot. But believe me the finest way to
arrive is by boat from seaward, for then you may appreciate just
why it has earned the reputation across the centuries for being one
of the loveliest and safest harbours of southwest England. On a
clear day you will pick up Berry Head to the north and Start Point
to the south, and there ahead are the steep tree-covered hills on both
flanks of the estuary with the two small, almost fairy-tale castles of
Dartmouth and Kingswear guarding the entrance. There is no
sandbank nor reef on which to founder, just the splendid deepwater
mouth with, at night, coloured leading lights to keep you on course
for a safe passage.

Old and new. Dartmouth higher ferry about 1912 ...

Dartmouth Castle, with St Petrox Church alongside, is in certain lights like some illustration from a children's history book. Built between 1481 and 1493 it was one of the first castles specially constructed to take cannon, and housed a battery of seven. Its basement is hewn out of the solid rock and the seven guns could splay the entrance with a deadly barrage of ball calculated to pierce the side of any enemy ship, or carry away the masts which was even more effective, for then the disabled vessel could be boarded and taken as a prize.

On the first floor were quarters for the garrison complete with fireplace and oven, and you may still examine the opening below the tower where, in 1488 a heavy barrier chain was installed to completely seal off the estuary mouth. The chain, later known as 'Jawbones' was attached to the rocks under Gommerock fort on the opposite bank, and at night was winched up taut. In the event of friendly ships needing to enter or leave, it was simply eased off to drop below the level of their keels.

But Dartmouth was an important harbour long before either the castles on Kingswear or Dartmouth side were built. A village which

. . . **and today.**

lay on the west bank at the time of the Norman Conquest was a
favoured embarkation and disembarkation point for Norman gentry
commuting between their French and English estates. It was from
here in 1147 that a fleet of 164 craft assembled in Warfleet Creek
just south of the present town for departure on the second Crusade.
How on earth they managed to anchor or moor that number of ships
in this small creek is a mystery to me. Granted the craft in those
days were tiny by modern standards, but even so I think they must
have been able to walk across a solid 'bridge' of ships from bank to
bank!

We know there was a church of some sort adjacent to Dartmouth
Castle as far back as 1192, for it is on record that a group of monks
were at that time under obligation to keep a lamp 'ever burning
before the altar of St Petrox'—possibly the first beacon ever lit at
the estuary mouth to assist ships approaching the coast at night. In
1347 Dartmouth sent 31 ships and 757 men to join the forces of
Edward III at the siege of Calais. In return for this, 30 years later
the town was raided and pillaged by the French, and it was from
that time that thoughts turned to the need for some form of

95

defences. In 1388 work was started on the fortifications but soon abandoned, not to be recommenced until 1481 when a grant was made by Edward IV who further decreed that the great barrier chain already mentioned be constructed.

Across history this has been a gathering-place for fleets, both naval and commercial, and today it is just as important, particularly in the latter respect although in a rather different field. The Darthaven Marina at Kingswear today has berths for some 235 craft, most of which berths are occupied all winter as a safe haven while 'laid-up-afloat'. Darthaven Marina was opened some ten years ago and is still feeling the need to extend its floating pontoons, for an enormous number of craft visit the harbour during a season. This is not surprising since Dartmouth lies almost exactly halfway between the Solent and Land's End.

There are, in addition, two other marinas in the harbour, both owned and run by the shipyard of Philip & Sons established in 1854 up at Noss Point. One of these, called the Kingswear Marina, is close alongside their shipyard at Noss Point, while the other is beneath the Britannia Naval College on the Dartmouth side. This latter marina has facilities for laying-up craft ashore, and is adjacent to the Dart Marina Hotel the manager of which told me that the hotel has the distinction of being the only hotel in the United Kingdom which is contracted out to be managed by Trust Houses Ltd. The hotel itself, like the Dart and Kingswear Marinas, is owned by Philip & Sons who also own and run the higher ferry. Altogether the three marinas, plus a number of much-prized deepwater moorings, do make Dartmouth a most desirable Mecca for yachtsmen.

Harbour Dues have to be paid by all vessels in, or visiting the port, of course. I chatted to Captain Moore MN, the Harbourmaster, in his office on South Embankment at Dartmouth, from whose window we could see literally hundreds of pleasure craft, as well as a flotilla of small fishing boats and the ever-present ferries crossing from side to side with their load of cars. It was a busy scene, all the more attractive because it lacked the industrial aspects which larger commercial vessels always bring with them such as docks, wharves and cranes. I asked him about the job of administering such a harbour.

'You may be sure', he told me, 'there is a waiting list for deepwater moorings out there, but I have to be very careful to ensure that the navigable channel is kept clear for ships going up to Totnes and Noss Point.

'We have one or two ships a month, of up to 1,000 tons displacement, going to Totnes,' he continued. 'They mostly go up to the Baltic Wharf below the bridge but vessels of over 240 feet in length and 12 feet draught are at risk due to the shallowing and bends in the river farther up. They come from Sweden, Finland and Russia, but the timber trade has fallen off lately somewhat. Of course we can take vessels up to 22,000 tons and 580 feet in length down here on the mainstream buoys.'

'About how many moorings, apart from the marinas, are there under your administration here?' I asked.

'1,800, give or take a few,' he told me. 'The Dart Harbour and Navigation Authority control the river up to the weir above Totnes—in fact as far as the tide flows into the estuary. We have responsibility for all the moorings, their chains and buoys, as well as the leading lights which keep vessels on a correct track at night when entering or leaving the entrance. We have no actual powers of arrest, as the police do, but we are backed up by Acts of Parliament and are wholly responsible for efficient administration of the river, and seeing that all parties have a fair share of the facilities. Did you say you had been canoeing up the river?'

I looked at the freckled face and twinkling brown eyes with a question in them. For a ghastly moment I thought he was going to impose Harbour Dues on my canoe, but his thoughts were elsewhere. 'Then doubtless you saw Sir Walter Raleigh's old boathouse just below the Anchor Stone?' I confirmed that I had indeed done so, and marvelled at the fine state of repair it was in. 'He used to soak the newly-cut masts for his ships in there,' Captain Moore laughed. 'Pickled the wood to make it last forever and remain supple. It took ages, but time must have passed more slowly in those days,' he chuckled.

'Do you manage to cater for all the requirements by yachtsmen in the height of the season?' I queried.

'More or less,' he responded. 'We have 200 names on the waiting list at the moment for permanent yacht moorings, but apart from that we can cope with it. We have two Trinity House Pilots operating here; have a word with David Griffiths the senior pilot, for he has just published a photographic book much of which deals with Dartmouth in the olden days.'

Castle Hotel and Quay 1865 . . .

So I winkled out David, and browsed through his excellent illustrated booklet entitled *A Century on the River Dart* which is published by the Museum, and we discussed seagoing traffic and trade, and the winds of change which had blown down the river across the years, and he told me of plans afoot to build quays at Noss Point large enough to accommodate vessels of 360 feet in length and it seemed to make him happier just to talk about it, which was quite understandable.

* * * * * *

During the last war the Britannia Royal Naval College was taken over by American forces in preparation for the combined assault on France. Hundreds of Combined Operations craft—Landing Craft Tank, Landing Craft Infantry, and the larger Landing Ships practised on nearby beaches along the coast. In the harbour concrete slipways were built—some of them are still in use—for the

. . . and 1986.

loading of tanks and other vehicles and personnel into the assault craft. The harbour throbbed with a tense activity and on the 6 June 1944, 480 assault and support craft sailed from Dartmouth to join a mighty Armada bound for the Normandy beaches.

But this harbour, owing to its very beautiful setting, has always attracted creative artists. In 1971 filming commenced here for that renowned BBC television series *'The Onedin Line'*, and few of the millions watching that fascinating epic imagined that the old port of Liverpool was in fact a modern Dartmouth having undergone some very clever 'plastic surgery' as you might say. Nor would they have suspected that those jungles of New Guinea were in fact Long Wood just up the creek above Noss Point!

You hobnob with history both fictional and real when you wander through the streets of the town today. Stand on the quayside and examine the Royal Castle Hotel. You are looking at a building which has gazed out over the river since 1639. Originally the hotel was four Tudor houses built on either side of a narrow lane just wide

enough to take a coach and horses, and it was not until 1835 that the well-known staircase and glass roof were added, making the roadway into the hotel foyer. Coaches served the hotel until 1911 and seven reigning monarchs have sojourned within its walls. Beams in the rooms are said to have been taken from wrecked ships of the Spanish Armada, and the famous Lydstone range in the Galleon Bar was forged in Dartmouth 300 years ago. It is still occasionally used. Compare the photograph taken from the Quay in 1865 with that taken in 1986, and you will see that under the superficial 'face lift' the frontage and bones of the place remain much as they have always been. But note the stone bridge on the extreme right of the old photograph and the masts of ships berthed in the area now taken by recreation gardens and a car park.

The small pleasure and fishing craft ranging at their mooring warps beneath your feet remind you that the Pilgrim Fathers in 1620, setting off for the New World in their somewhat leaky *Mayflower* and *Speedwell* from Southampton put into this harbour while repairs were effected to *Speedwell*. They gained the Scilly Isles but had to return to Plymouth for further repairs and provisioning before finally leaving our shores.

When you pass along the beautifully preserved seventeenth-century Butterwalk, remember that it was here in number 6 that Charles II is reputed to have held court. The building is now the Borough Museum. Turn into Foss Street and look toward the church; you will not find it all that much altered from how it must have looked 200 years ago. Alas, the very beautiful old building I have sketched was destroyed by a bomb during the last war, though you may still see one of the original pilaster buttresses high up the wall.

Leave your car behind, and walk southward down the incomparable quay stretching from higher ferry into the town, and for real value do it at evening when the setting sun is tinting the rocks at the harbour mouth russet and gold, backed by the steep green slopes of Mount Ridley beyond Kingswear. When the lights come on in the town it is magical. Dartmouth Castle and the church of St Petrox will be silhouetted against the horizon of sea beyond, dark in the shadows of Gallant's Bower. Walk through South Town

Left: Foss Street. 1900. This beautiful building was destroyed by a bomb in the last war.

101

Below right: Dartmouth from Gallant's Bower. A
very early engraving now exhibited in Badgers Holt
at Dartmeet. Above: Dartmouth at evening—the
castle and St Petrox Church silhouetted against
the horizon.

to that promontory, and as you steadily rise look back and down at
the river with a myriad boats snug inside. It is a scene of surpassing
beauty; an altogether fitting culmination of a wonderful river in a
pastoral jewel of a harbour.

I stood above the castle one summer evening as boats from the
Naval College were entering the Narrows from seaward, their wakes
wide 'V's in the calm water. Following them came a handful of
pleasure yachts, their sails almost limp in the dying breeze. Far cry,
I thought, looking down at the dark green water which was just
about to start ebbing again out to sea... a far cry from that lonely
windswept crown up there on Dartmoor where it all began. Yet
somewhere mingling with those salty depths was that chuckling
brown peaty flow of Broad Marsh and Sandy Hole Pass. More than
45 miles it has travelled, as we have, to this point.

Flanked in turn by grass, heather and fern, green conifers and broadleaved woods, farmlands and landscaped estates, it has finally arrived rich in experience at these rocky outcrops of our coast which are glowing gold in the sunset. Serving, and in turn being served by the terrain through which it passes, the river has grown in stature and beauty and given us much in the process.

We owe it a debt.

Let us hope that we, and future generations, will repay that debt by keeping it pure and unpolluted so that in the years ahead it will speak to them as it speaks to us today.

The Word's Answer

Oh, rose is the colour of love and youth,
And green is the colour of faith and truth
And brown of the fruitful clay.
The earth is fruitful, and faithful, and young,
And her bridal morn shall rise ere long,
And you shall know what the rocks and the streams
And the laughing greenwoods say!

Charles Kingsley

ALSO AVAILABLE

COASTLINE OF
CORNWALL
by Ken Duxbury

SEA STORIES OF
CORNWALL
by Ken Duxbury

HISTORIC INNS OF DEVON
by Monica Wyatt

CASTLES OF DEVON
by James Mildren

WESTCOUNTRY
HAUNTINGS
by Peter Underwood

SECRET WESTCOUNTRY
by Rosemary Clinch, Hilary
Wreford & Michael Williams

E V THOMPSON'S
WESTCOUNTRY

PEOPLE & PLACES
IN DEVON
by Monica Wyatt

MYSTERIES IN THE
DEVON LANDSCAPE
by Hilary Wreford &
Michael Williams

SEA STORIES OF DEVON
Introduced by E V Thompson

DARTMOOR IN THE
OLD DAYS
by James Mildren

AROUND GLORIOUS
DEVON
by David Young

WESTCOUNTRY
MYSTERIES
Introduced by Colin Wilson

UNKNOWN DEVON
by Rosemary Anne Lauder
Monica Wyatt &
Michael Williams

GHOSTS OF DEVON
by Peter Underwood

LEGENDS OF DEVON
by Sally Jones

DARTMOOR PRISON
by Rufus Endle

EXMOOR IN THE
OLD DAYS
by Rosemary Anne Lauder

UNKNOWN BRISTOL
by Rosemary Clinch

GHOSTS OF SOMERSET
by Peter Underwood

We shall be pleased to send you our catalogue giving full details of our growing list of titles for Devon, Cornwall and Somerset and forthcoming publications.

If you have difficulty in obtaining our titles, write direct to Bossiney Books, Land's End, St Teath, Bodmin, Cornwall.